The Head of the Family

CLAYTON C. BARBEAU

The Liturgical Press

Collegeville   Minnesota

ISBN: 0-8146-0901-5

Contents

Introduction

PRIMITIVE men forged varied stories about their origins and the creation of the world. For some, the world was the result of a struggle between two deities, one of whom became enmeshed in matter. For others, the earth was formed with arduous labor by several gods out of raw matter. Today, some men maintain that the universe and human life are the result of a chain of accidents—always presupposing, of course, an existing matter that could be involved in an accident. Standing tall and luminous above these myths is the first sentence of the book of Genesis: "God, at the beginning of time, created heaven and earth." God. Not two or twenty, but one God. Not an accident, a collision in space, but God. There is no hint of struggle, no arduous toil, just the calm statement that God "created heaven and earth." As we read further in the creation story, we see that God, by the mere act of His will, out of all the fruitfulness of His Being, created all that is, and all that He made He found "good." "God made man in his own image, made him in the image of God. Man and woman both, he created them. And God pronounced his blessing on them, increase and multiply and fill the earth, and make it yours; take command of the fishes in the sea, and all that flies through the air, and all the living things that move on the earth." (Gen. 1:27-28)

The relationship of God the Creator to his children is that of a father. The Old Testament writers, however, give us only hints of the Divine Paternity. They saw that God had created the universe, had "fathered" it and that He

continued to care for it. They recognized paternal solicitude in that act of the Lord for His first fallen creatures:
"And now the Lord provided garments for Adam and his
wife, made out of skins, to clothe them." (Gen. 3:21)
Again and again, the image of the careful father is used to
depict God's care for His creatures: ". . . the Lord your
God carried you through the desert as a man carries his
little son . . . And dost thou doubt that the Lord is chas-
tening thee, as a man chastens his own son, training thee
to keep the commandments of the Lord thy God, and
follow the path he chooses, and live in fear of him?"
(Deut. 1:31, 8:5) But while using figurative language
which described God's loving treatment as that of a
father, no writer before the time of Christ dared to
claim that our relationship to God was that of sons to
father. Such a statement would have been impossible.
God's Fatherhood is rooted not in creation but in His
eternal generation of His Only Begotten Son. Only the Son
could truly say "Father."

Our Lord's first recorded statement is that which he
made when Mary and Joseph found Him in the temple:
"Could you not tell that I must needs be in the place
which belongs to my Father?" (Luke 2:49) The name of
the Father was constantly on His lips, in all His preach-
ings, in the Sermon on the Mount, in His agony in the
garden; and we who before His coming could not say "my
Father," He taught to say "Our Father." St. Paul tells us
that through Christ we are "all now God's sons," (Gal.
3:26) and, moved by the spirit of our adoption, we can
now "cry out, Abba, Father." (Rom. 8:16) It is only
through the Son that the fatherhood of God is extended to
us; through Him the Father of the Word has become our
Father. Our Lord underscored this at the time of His
resurrection: "I am going up to him who is my Father and
your Father, who is my God and your God." (John 20:17)

Our heavenly Father is not to be approached except
through Christ: "I am the way; I am truth and life; no-
body can come to the Father, except through me. If you

had learned to recognize me, you would have learned to recognize my Father too. From now onwards you are to recognize him; you have seen him." (John 14:6) As Pope John XXIII told his clergy during his patriarchate at Venice: "Jesus is the way. He is the supreme gift of the Father. For the Christian what matters is to be incorporated in Christ, and to be united to Him. The Son of God will make each baptized person a member of His Body, setting up a family relationship, that of a son, between him and his heavenly Father. This way of expressing it was so dear to St. Paul that he used it 164 times in his letters." God's paternity is made manifest, Pope John concluded, in the Church where "In His Son, made man, the heavenly Father calls his creatures to life with him as in a family."

This family finds its source at the baptismal font where the child is blessed by the hands of Christ and under the sign of the Blessed Trinity born into a new life—a life that is protected and nourished to its fulness by the Church whose ministers, with real paternal love, feed their children on the Bread of Life, guide and instruct them in the paths of righteousness. Thus, the celibate priest knows a true fatherhood as profound as any experience by the man who has physically fathered a family. His solicitude and constant loving concern for those under his care is at the heart of any definition of true paternity.

The act of engendering a new child—the greatest of man's privileges—may make a man an actual father but not a true one. The mere breeding of young does not constitute true paternity. Our servicemen overseas have left behind them hundreds of thousands of children whom they have actually fathered, but true fatherhood is not theirs. So, too, with the "unwed fathers" at home who, even if aware of the consequences of their acts, have accepted no responsibility for their children. This notion of responsibility is at the crux of true paternity.

The conscious sense of responsibility for the physical and spiritual well-being of others is the mark of a true father. It was in this sense that Joseph was the father of Jesus. "Think, of what anguish of mind thy father and I have endured, searching for thee" (Luke 2:48) the Virgin Mary said to the Child Jesus. Joseph is the exemplar of all who are true fathers, whether childless or not, who exert their energies, devote their time and efforts, even endure "anguish of mind" in guiding and caring for the young around them. They console, advise, assist, admonish, and deeply cherish all those who have need of them.

We have all had experience of such a person as this: the professor to whom youngsters in trouble feel they can turn with a fuller confidence than they might have in their own fathers; the childless uncle who stands quietly in the background of family gatherings, but is never unaware of the needs of his nephews and nieces. Such men as these are true fathers, showing forth a love and a generosity totally free of any thought of return: a pale image, but an image indeed, of the loving Fatherhood of God.

Once having recognized that true paternity is not necessarily allied with fatherhood in the flesh—which we have chosen to call actual fatherhood—it is but a short step to the realization that all men are, by reason of their very masculinity, called to be true fathers. The acceptance of responsibility for others, especially those too weak to stand yet alone, the solicitude for their spiritual and physical good rooted in a love devoid of selfishness, this paternity is the crown of manhood, the insignia of a man's maturity.

Our concern here, however, is limited to a consideration of those of us who are actually fathers in the flesh and also are striving to become true fathers as well. Ours is a daily struggle to transform, in response to the graces we have received, our fatherhood in the flesh into a real fatherhood in spirit also.

This emphasis upon a relationship in spirit being superior to a relationship in the flesh must not be misunderstood. The union of man and woman in the flesh, "the blessing which alone was not taken away in punishment for original sin nor the doom of the flood," as the traditional Nuptial Blessing reminds us, is a union willed by God. It was God who created sex; it was God who chose in this fashion to give man a share in his own creative power and who ordained that the conjugal act should be a source of intense pleasure. Indeed, St. Thomas points out that the pleasure attached to sex was probably more intense, the whole experience richer, before the fall.

For those puritans who think that the marriage act is somehow ugly and unworthy of God we might recall Père Roguet's words: "Human generation, the fruit of marriage, was willed by God who, on the evening of the sixth day, after creating man and woman and ordering them to multiply, said not only that it was 'good,' as he had said of all the previous creations, but that it was 'very good,' (Gen. 1:31) that is to say very beautiful, very holy, truly worthy of himself."

Chapter I

THE FATHER AS CREATOR

"(Parents) should realize that they are thereby co-operators with the love of God the Creator, and are, so to speak, the interpreters of that love. Thus they will fulfil their task with human and Christian responsibility, and, with docile reverence toward God, will make decisions by common counsel and effort. Let them thoughtfully take into account both their own welfare and that of their children, those already born and those which the future may bring . . . Thus, trusting in divine Providence and refining the spirit of sacrifice married Christians glorify the Creator and strive toward fulfilment in Christ when with a generous human and Christian sense of responsibility they acquit themselves of the duty to procreate."

(Church in the modern world, No. 50).

THE MARRIAGE vow is a creative vow in the fullest sense of that term. It is a vow that joins this man and this woman in a relationship stronger than any other and, indeed, creates an indissoluble union.

The union that is marriage is stronger even than the ties that bind parent to child. "That is why a man is destined to leave father and mother, and cling to his wife instead, so that the two become one flesh." (Gen. 2:24) If a man's parents seek to prevent or undermine his marriage, that leaving of father and mother can be taken in its most severe sense.

A man must be free to marry or not to marry, but once his choice is made, once his pledge of fidelity is given, there is no return. He and his wife are now "one flesh." Their union is—and has been since the creation of mankind—a union willed by God and cannot be sundered by any man. No longer do they belong to themselves, for they have vowed themselves to each other. They have given themselves away, "he, not she, claims the right over her body, as she, not he, claims the right over his." (I Cor. 7:4) And like that other Christian paradox—that only he who "loses his life" shall save it—this giving, too, reaps a rich return, for in giving themselves away, each gains the other. When this giving is done by two who are married "in the Lord," (I Cor. 7:39) then it is Christ's own love that each gives and receives.

But the union of man and wife does not dissolve their personal identities. Their marriage vow is not a magic formula that wipes away all that marks them as unique persons. It does not replace their separate personalities with a neuter "we" that is neither the husband's nor the wife's personality. The "we" must indeed be created out of the love of each for the other, but the man and the woman must both work to create this "we." They must labor to bring into being this new personality, a personality that expresses their oneness, a personality that is larger and richer than that which either could know alone. For the woman is helping—by her submissiveness, by her love, by her need for this person, her dependence upon him—to bring her husband to maturity. And the husband—by his fidelity, by his tender care and his strong leadership—is bringing alive in his wife the fulness of her womanhood. This is something that may be accomplished consciously or unconsciously, though too much self-consciousness about the mutation that is being worked out can be as harmful as being totally unaware that such a mutation is meant to come about.

What both husband and wife must know is that their life together will be one long creative endeavor to fulfill the other, to unfold tenderly in the other all of the good that the lover has seen there, to let it flourish in an atmosphere of love and appreciation.

What too often happens is quite the reverse. Each party comes to the marriage radiant with the belief that this other person is going to heal all of his or her physical and mental aches and pains and is quite surprised to discover, not too much later, that the other has aches and pains of his or her own. This leads to disillusionment, to bitterness, the feeling that one has been unfairly "trapped" by sexual desire or the wiles of the other party, often followed by recriminations, arguments or embittered silence and the bearing of a sometimes lifelong grudge.

How different though that marriage which is founded upon a true love for the other, a constant desire to protect and feed and keep healthy the happiness of the other. Such a marriage cannot become the vicious snake of disillusion eating its own bitter tail of dissatisfaction. Such a marriage rooted in mutual love becomes a creation of marvelous beauty, with each party seeking new ways of expressing the love and happiness he or she knows. Every sort of symbolism comes into play here, the world becomes rich with unexpected surprises. The canvas of marriage becomes glorious with one shared experience following another; each tries to outdo the other in finding new ways to express their love. The early verbalizing, the magic and romantic lyricism of love letters is left behind and even the constant repetition of the words of love finds husband and wife admitting to each other that words do not express what they wish them to express. Verbal symbols give way to a thousand variations of concrete symbols —a "surprise" gift, a note in the refrigerator, an evening planned totally for the other—always designed to unlock in the other that secret closet of joy. In creating their masterpiece, truly "their life's work," the husband and the wife each look to the other's needs. Each seeks to understand the other as a person, to meet and respond to the call of the other at each given moment.

For the man this demands not only a knowledge of what it is he has married—a woman—but whom he has married, this very personal woman. The husband must drop his easy assumptions and superficial estimates of "women" and truly seek to understand just in what way it is that this woman is meant to be dependent and submissive and what this entails from him. "You, too, who are husbands must use marriage considerately," St. Peter tells us, "paying homage to woman's sex as weaker than your own." (I Peter 3:7) He must struggle to awaken in her that desire for dependence and submission, and work with a real skill to bring to flower her womanhood. As Father Theodore Mackin wrote: "A woman's submission in the experience of marriage is not equivalent to the unconditional surrender of a defeated enemy. It is rather her taking the specifically feminine role in experiences that cannot have place at all unless she brings something positive and valuable to them. A husband's artistry lies partly in bringing her talents into play, in making her consistently more woman and wife by perfecting the girl."

Marriage then is a creative work. Both parties must labor to make a beautiful marriage. The wreckage of the miserable marriages we see all about us today is due mainly to this: that one or the other or both of the parties did not know that to make a marriage work means to work at making a marriage. Often enough, if only one party is willing to work, to continue to sacrifice, the marriage can at least be rescued from disaster if not transformed. St. Peter's advice to the wives of pagan husbands fits equally well the circumstances of husbands whose wives are less than Christian: "win them over, not by word but by example; by the modesty and reverence they observe in your demeanour." (I Peter 3:2)

In the communion of conjugal love the marriage act is at once the most beautiful and the most underrated of communications. Underrated because, while our society is full of throbbing sexuality, there is hardly any knowledge or appreciation of the meaning and purpose of sex. To see sex as mere thrill or pleasure, even as the highest pleasure, is to underestimate sex. Of all the means of communicating love that are open to husband and wife, the sexual act is the most perfect. For either party to seek from it only personal satisfaction is to destroy the richest symbol of mutual love that a man and a wife have. The man who peeled the banana, ate the skin and threw the banana away was always good for a laugh in vaudeville, and yet he was doing only what the thrill seeker is doing.

The real substance of the marriage act is the mutual love it expresses. That is what is so tragic about all of the books on sexual technique advertised in our press. No amount of "technique" can enrich the marriage act that is not first an act of love. On the contrary, a mutual love and a mutual desire to bring and give to the other one's whole person will bring about a profusion of gestures, caresses and other expressions of love so rich and so unselfconscious that one could only degrade them by calling them a "technique."

The husband, again, should assume the major responsibility for the success of the marriage act. While his whole masculine nature seems to orient him for rapid conquest, the husband should remember that his wife's feminine nature will normally seek from him assurances of his tender and constant love before she gives herself away. It cannot be stressed too much that the tone of the sexual experience is different for men and for women and that, while the experience may be emotionally slight in a man, it is quite profound in most women. It requires only a little experience of a husband who is shallow enough to look upon sex as a mere thrill for himself for a wife to close off from him that which is authentically herself in the marriage act. In this sense the act becomes one-sided. He is using her body. She denies him her person.

In a relationship, however, where the husband and wife look upon the marriage act as a symbol of their total commitment to one another, where neither the husband's brutality or shallowness nor the wife's frigidity mar it, where the husband has tenderly awakened in his wife that confidence in his love that her whole being demands, then the act assumes the stature of another creation. In such a happy case, love making does just that: it makes more love. The marriage act becomes the positive, dynamic symbol of the interpenetration of their lives and personalities. It may be a major symbol, but it is not the only one. The marriage act is part of the continent of their life together, not an island separated from their daily work.

We shall discuss in future pages the even greater symbolism of this union, but here we are restricting ourselves to the creative element in marriage and family life. Procreation means to create on behalf of. Men are allowed to create on behalf of heaven. The children born to men are meant for eternal life. The marriage act is thus the ultimate creative act of a man. By it, men are allowed to create the bodies of human persons, bodies which are destined for resurrection and eternity. All of Michelangelo's creations—the frescos in the Sistine Chapel, the dome of St. Peter's, the great works of sculpture for Pope Julius's tomb—all of the magnificent outpourings of a creative genius are not worth one baby. And Michelangelo could not alone produce a baby.

If the love of a man and woman which expresses itself in the creation of a hundred symbols of love is to express itself in a child, God must be there. Earthly fatherhood is impossible without the direct intervention of the Father of All. It is only by His divine act that a human soul is infused into the joined seed of the parents. It is only by His infusion of the soul that a new human person will result from the physical act of the parents, a person of intelligence and will, reflecting God's own image and destined for immortal life with Him. "Then thou sendest forth thy spirit," the Psalmist sang, "and there is fresh creation; thou dost repeople the face of earth." (Psalm 103:30)

If a couple's love is to be fruitful, if they are to incarnate their love in a third person (in a marvelous imaging of the Blessed Trinity) then their love must be triune. The Father must bend to them and breathe the "breath of life" into their joined seed. The marriage act, every time it is performed, is a word uttered into the night, a prayer that God bless this union with the word that is the "breath of life," indeed, life itself. The union of man and wife which is a union in Christ is a form of worship. In giving themselves to each other in the sacrament, they are giving themselves to Christ. The Rite of Matrimony according to English usage recognizes this fact with the phrase: "With my body I thee worship."

Even when the union is not creative in the bodily sense, the union is yet immeasurably richer than any mere "thrill-seeker" can imagine. The marriage act, when it symbolizes the union of Christ and His Church, is a symbolizing that communicates grace. The husband and wife become channels of grace for each other in this act. Having chosen to live within the sacrament of marriage, a husband and wife have chosen to live not only intimately with each other, but in intimacy with God. "The grace of eternal life belongs to both," St. Peter says. (I Peter 3:7) One of the richest springs of this divine life for each other will be the marriage act; their conjugal union is the living out of their specific holiness; and Christian holiness is growth in a specific sacramental role which is part of the larger drama that is the life of the Church.

The marriage act, therefore, is not only the source of new human life and deepening of human love, it is meant to be a source of that "more abundant life," of growth in the Divine love-life. In the Constitution on the Church: the Fathers state: "Authentic married love is caught up into divine love and is governed and enriched by Christ's redeeming power and the saving activity of the Church. Thus, this love can lead the spouses to God with powerful effect and can aid and strengthen them in the sublime office of being a father or a mother." (Pastoral Constitution on the Church in the Modern World, p. 48)

The commitment husband and wife make to one another, then, is creative. It is the necessary condition for the full flowering of their love-life. It permits them experiences of a quality impossible to those who do not enjoy the freedom that flows from the vows, the openness that springs from an unquestioned fidelity to the other.

Even as those who have grounded their marriage in this sacred territory are open to each other, so do they strive to remain open to all others—especially to the children of their love. Such men know what the Psalmist felt when he sang: "Thy wife shall be fruitful as a vine, in the heart of thy home, the children round thy table sturdy as olive-branches" (Psalm 127:3). The true father sees himself neither as bound down by his children, nor as one ensnared by forces beyond his control, but as a man the Lord would use to further enrich creation. He sees himself as a man through whom the almighty Creator has chosen to work and his children as mysteries, persons willed by God to fulfill a place not to be decided by the father but by and through the grace of God himself. With the Psalmist this father can sing: "Fatherhood itself is the Lord's gift, the fruitful womb is a reward that comes from him. Crown of thy youth, children are like arrows in a warrior's hand. Happy, whose quiver is filled with these. . . ." (Psalm 126:3-5)

Only God can create out of nothing. Only God can cause something to exist by the mere act of His will. For man, even in his "garden of delight," it would have been necessary that he have something to work on or with if he was to make something new. Thus, if he were to make a vase, he must have clay to mould. If he was to whittle a lyre, he must have wood to whittle on and a knife to whittle with. Yet God gave to man a share in his creative work, a higher share than any other creature. He gave man the power to provide the bodies of new persons—bodies which He would quicken into life with a soul. Now this is the closest that man can come to the creativity of God, to share in God's creative activity in this way. It is the great blessing of God upon us—and even if it is mitigated by the consequences of Original Sin it remains a blessing still. Eve herself sang a hymn of joy at the birth of her first child, "I have been enriched by the Lord with a man-child." (Gen. 4:1) And our Lord said: "A woman in childbirth feels distress, because now her time has come; but when she was borne her child, she does not remember the distress any longer, so glad is she that a man has been born into the world." (John 16:21)

It is in the womb of woman that the body of man is fashioned. Her role results in profound physical changes that work slowly at the very core of her life as a woman. The basic cycle of her physical life changes, her breasts grow tender as they ripen, the child in her womb draws from her body its sustenance, grows larger, moves about. She bears within her the incalculable treasure, patiently she awaits the "fulness of time." Her close contact with the mystery is full of a meaning she cannot utter. At the center of her being is a rich pool of silence, the silence of communion, reverent and joyful. It is a silence akin to the silence of heaven when the seventh seal was opened for the seal of a new life has opened within her, and the vision cannot be uttered.

The father has no such experience of his paternity. Indeed, the unique act whereby he generated this particular child is probably lost for him in the past. It is an effort for him to grasp his responsibility for the transformation taking place in his spouse. Rarely will his sense of fatherhood blossom within him before the birth of the child, before it is free of its mother and visibly belonging to both of them. Even then his recognition of his parenthood will be a gradual enlightment. The mother, in most cases, will continue to meet all the child's needs, to care for it, change it, to feed it with the food of her breasts. But the father will already be beginning to glimpse his new style of being. His bride has become a mother. He has fulfilled in her what was only a potentiality and by making that potentiality an actuality he has made himself a father. His relationship to his wife is now richer than when he was only her husband; he is now the father of their child. She is now a mother and in the first months of her new motherhood she will have need of him in different ways than ever before. New depths of tenderness and solicitude which he called forth out of her must now be met by an equal tenderness and solicitude on his part. He has called forth a new woman, a mother, and now she calls forth a new man, a father. Theirs is no longer merely the relationship of husband and wife, for their mutual love has been blessed by God and is now embodied in a new person, the person of their child. Each has given to the other the image of their love. The ineffable, the unutterable feelings each had tried falteringly to communicate to the other —and never adequately expressed—are now embodied. The child is the personification of their love.

This would be mystery enough, even if it were all. For who can comprehend how the mutual love of a man and a woman could become incarnate? But this is not all. The mystery is but a symbol of the greatest of mysteries, the mystery of the inner life of God Himself. For in every human family we have only feeble images of the Blessed Trinity. God the Father from all eternity has generated His Son and the mingling of their mutual love is the Person of the Holy Spirit. The Father is truly Father, the Son is truly Son; theirs is indeed a relationship of paternity and filiation, a relationship that is the ground out of which all created relationships of fatherhood and sonship spring. "I fall on my knees," St. Paul wrote, "to the Father of our Lord Jesus Christ, that Father from whom all fatherhood in heaven and earth takes its title." (Eph. 3:14-15)

To share in God's own creation of new life is the greatest blessing of all—a privilege even the angels do not enjoy— and yet this does not end the creative activity required of man and wife. The birth of their child requires from the parents a new endeavor: they must set about to build a temple for this new image of God, they must give a home to the child.

Even as God's creation images Him, so our homes will image us. We are all familiar with homes where the overflow of love is like a warm hearth. As one little Italian lady said to a prospective tenant looking at a large flat with only one heater: "Ah, but a large family warms a house." We are also familiar with the sterile chill of those homes where a mutual distrust, a certain fear of each other and of life itself has led to a cold-bloodedness that is like a constant draught from some dark cellar.

The home, the home-life, the family itself, will reflect the spirit and love-artistry of both husband and wife; but, before God, it is the head of the house who will be held chiefly responsible for this whole creation. It is always salutary for the fathers of families to recall that it was Eve who first ate of the fruit—and that absolutely nothing happened. Eve did not head the human race. But when she talked Adam into taking a bite—well, we are all too aware of the consequences of that pathetically masculine act.

In creating the home we should keep in mind that ideally the family home is just that—a family home. It should be stable, solid; a home must be somewhere before it can be something. Stable people are the products of stable homes. The person "at home" in the world is generally the one who has a home in the world. Today some men endanger their marriages, the souls of their children and the happiness of their families by accepting as a "fact of life"—if they want to "succeed"—the need for constant transfers, for movement hither and yon. But "success" for the Christian must be measured in other terms than those of the contemporary corporation. A man does not sacrifice the greater for the less.

This creation of the home life which seems to demand the stability of a home is the basic concern of the father. He it is who must decide where the family shall live and how he is to provide for it. Compromises will often be necessary in this matter; we must live in this society. Only the father will know what was a necessary compromise and what was a capitulation to the social drift—only he and God.

When the home, for some fundamental reason, lacks that stability, the father must strive even harder to make the family itself an anchor for his children. So long as the life within is stable, ordered, full of mutual love and respect—a true family life—the home could be a flat, a tent. The wandering Jews of the past, the wandering Arabs of today, have this sort of stability, this strong family loyalty. Family life of such substance is not accidental. It does not merely happen as children are born, but must be consciously worked at by the parents. Again, it is a creation in the fullest sense. The family is a work of art, a mosaic of the mutual love and respect of husband, wife and children, a mosaic illumined by Him who called Himself the "Light."

The father, then, is first of all one who is and knows

himself to be responsible for creation and, in many ways, is himself a creator. But he must never forget that it is only in Christ and through Christ that any creation at all is possible: "It was through him that all things came into being, and without him came nothing that has come to be." (John 1:3)

Chapter II

THE FATHER AS LOVER

"When there is (a) question of harmonizing conjugal love with the responsible transmission of life, the moral aspect of any procedure does not depend solely on sincere intentions or on an evaluation of motives, but must be determined by objective standards. These, based on the nature of the human person and his acts preserve the full sense of mutual self-giving and human procreation in the context of true love. Such a goal cannot be achieved unless the virtue of conjugal chastity is sincerely practised . . . All should be persuaded that human life and the task of transmitting it are not realities bound up with this world alone. Hence they cannot be measured or perceived only in terms of it, but always have a bearing on the eternal destiny of men."

(*Church in the modern world, No. 51*).

"Marriage to be sure is not instituted solely for procreation; rather, its very nature as an unbreakable compact between persons, and the welfare of the children, both demand that the mutual love of the spouses be embodied in a rightly ordered manner, that it grow and ripen. Therefore, marriage persists as a whole manner and communion of life, and maintains its value and indissolubility, even when despite the often intense desire of the couple, offspring are lacking."

(*Church in the modern world, No. 50*).

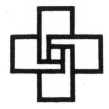

In St. Matthew, Christ says: "Thou shalt love thy neighbor as thyself." (Matt. 22:40) And St. Paul tells us that this statement is a summing up of all the commandments. (Rom. 13:8-9)

"As thyself . . ." How aware we are of ourselves! Our own feelings, hopes, fears, memories, troubles and joys are constantly with us, thrusting themselves like barricades between our deepest selves and others. We are always on the lookout to protect our interests, to care for our persons, our reputations, to protect our property. Above all we are always quick to make excuses for our blunders, to give the best possible interpretations for our actions. "Now, look at it from my point of view . . ." and "But you've got to understand my position . . ." are phrases often on our lips. No man, not even the murderer or the suicide means to will himself evil. The murderer sees his crime as benefiting himself somehow, and the suicide sees his death as a good opposed to some evil which he thinks is greater. We will our own good, that is part of our nature.

But what is love? Ultimately, love is a mystery and an all-encompassing definition is impossible. St. Thomas, however, offers us the best working definition, and when he tells us that to love is to will the good of the other, he is echoing our Lord's own words. This definition includes two important points which require elaboration. The first of these is that love pertains not so much to the emotions or the sexual appetite as to the will.

It is the will, informed by the intellect, that chooses to love or not to love. True love between a man and a woman rules out neither the physical nor the emotional, but subordinates these faculties to man's judgment and will. Only the clear realization that love is a matter of the will can help us avert the tragedy that follows the belief that love is solely a matter of the emotions or of physical desire. Actually, physical and emotional attachments are deepened and strengthened with the passage of time if there is true love.

The contemporary insanity about sex, marriage and family life, the personal misery of millions of our fellow human beings are consequences of giving the wrong answer to the question, "What is love?" There is a rather widespread belief that love is the desire for sexual union with another person. That love and sexual passion are not the same we have partially indicated in the previous chapter when we pointed out that the sexual act is but one method of communicating love. Trying to found love on physical desire alone is like trying to plant a tree on the surface of a raging sea. Should love depend upon physical desire, then it is doomed to die when physical desire fades away—and illness or accident in a moment can wipe away the basis of that desire. And most certainly the strongest of passionate desires is diminished when the desired object is attained and each day becomes more familiar—unless love is present. Is it too much of an oversimplification to say that the divorce courts are full of people who married thinking that the physical excitement aroused by the other was love and who after a year or two of marriage has caused that physical passion to subside have convinced themselves that their love has died? One woman, after her fourteenth divorce, announced she was still seeking the "right man." She cannot find him because no human being can keep physical passion alive while at the same time quenching it.

More prevalent than the confusion of love with physical desire is the notion that love is an irresistible emotional force against which the human being cannot stand. According to the simplifications of our contemporary folklore, especially of our literature and entertainment media, love is liable to strike us at any moment like a crippling disease—given the virus of the right object. Those screen lovers who wail "I can't help myself," or "There's nothing I can do," and, alas, those influenced by them would make of love such a sickness. To say that this emotional state is love, however, is to identify love with something in our nature even more unpredictable than physical desire. Our emotional states vary from day to day, hour to hour; our moods change, our gaiety today may give way to tomorrow's sadness. No man laughs all day and, equally, no man could long sustain the high pitched emotional frenzy that some would tell us constitutes love.

These two errors about love—that it is physical desire or an emotional state, or a combination of the two—both make the same mistake of explaining love in terms of what it does to the individual who feels the emotion or knows the passion; they look inward to the "lover" and not outward to the "beloved." Further, they would place love outside of the control of the person loving and, in so doing, rob it of its most precious attribute.

The very reason love is priceless is because it is free. That love which is not freely given is not love at all. Nothing can compel us to love another person. God Himself does not compel us to love Him. Love is totally under our control. If it were not, then our Lord could not have commanded us to love for He would have been commanding us to do something beyond our powers. Yet, He did command us to love, and in a certain way. "Thou shalt love thy neighbor as thyself."

When the free choice of our wills to unite our lives with another person is armoured with the vow of lifelong fidelity and further protected by a chaste heart, it is capable of weathering all the storms of time and circumstance. Such a love can withstand even the emotional or physical attraction of another who might seem to promise us more in return for our love. Though our present condition be miserable and a change of partners seems to offer immense advantages, we have but to look to the Christ who died a miserable death on the cross in order to know what love can demand.

"To will the good of the *other*." There is no hint here of any return to the lover. That is what we mean when we say that love is ecstatic—that all flows out to the other. True, we do in actual fact often seek a return of love, often seek a reward, but to the degree that this is so, there is a dilution of the purity of the love; and if ever our love craves only possession of the beloved, then it has given way to lust. If we want the good of the other only because that good will redound to our own benefit, then our love has become covetousness. Both of these falsifications of love result in a depersonalization of the beloved. We strip the beloved of her subjectivity, we no longer see her as a person, but look upon her simply as some object having reference only to ourselves. We begin to look upon her as important because of that relationship she has to us, some use we might put her to, rather than as one precious and unique and to be loved for what she is in herself.

Gabriel Marcel, the French philosopher, is especially rich in insights into the problems of our age. Like many other writers, theologians and psychologists, Marcel speaks of the need for us to strive to allow others to be "present" for us in such a way that we see these others not in relationship to ourselves, or for some use we might put them to, but as they see themselves. Marcel uses the term "presence" when speaking of this, of our being present for others, of others being present for us.

Another philosopher-theologian, Martin Buber, had a crucial experience which radically changed his outlook upon the world, an experience which gives us an indication of what this sort of presence entails. One day a young man came to Buber with a few questions. The philosopher was polite, answered the young man's questions, was no more, no less friendly than he would have been with any other of his students, and the young man departed. The young man went out and committed suicide. The news of the death made Buber profoundly aware of the fact that the young man had not been really "present" for him during the interview. He, Buber, had been courteous enough, had answered the student's questions patiently, but had failed to take enough interest in his visitor to see him as a person, to really see that the young man was troubled by larger, unasked questions. Buber later learned that it was those very unasked questions that the young man had hoped would be answered—Buber had been the student's last resort and Buber had failed.

A clipping on my desk from a recent newspaper gives another example of the turning of a person into an object. A young man called his psychoanalyst to inform him that he had slashed his wrists in an attempt at suicide and to beg the psychoanalyst please to come by and see him. The doctor is quoted as having replied that it "would not be good professional conduct to see a patient under such circumstances" and as having told the young man to go get first aid and come to his office for an appointment the next day. This young man, like Buber's student, succeeded in committing suicide. Whether or not it would have been good professional conduct, might it not have been good human conduct to have gone to the aid of the young man? The fact that a man is a "patient" should not make us forget that he is, first of all, a human being.

All of us can profit by these examples. How often in our own home life do we not tend to look upon our wives and our children as objects—"the wife," "the kids"—rather than as unique beings each possessed of his or her own inviolate personality. Often we do not realize that we have turned them into objects until some crisis arises, some tragedy, which jolts us awake, making us realize that we do not *own* this other person, that he or she is capable of being lost to us, that he or she has hidden depths that we shall never know, that he or she can suffer while we can do little about it. How often do we really only tend to care for another, to be "care-full" about another, to "will the good of the other"—in short, to love another—when some such crisis as sickness or accident has jolted us awake.

In some homes the crisis is not sickness or accident, but the result of the revolt of a human spirit against such depersonalization. Not too long ago a young girl, described as a good student and a normal youngster, sat in the front room of her home with a loaded .22 rifle on her lap. When her fourteen year old brother entered the house, she shot him dead. Her mother was at work, so was her father. She sat down to await their arrival so that she might kill them before killing herself. When her mother came up the path, the girl panicked and gave up her scheme. Questioned, she gave as her motive for the crime the fact that everything was so "dull." Her mother and her father went off to work in the morning, she and her brother went to school; they all came home in the evening, ate their evening meal, watched TV a little and went to bed in order to wake up the next morning and start the same routine over again. If that was life, she felt, let's have done with it.

This child's reaction was tragically drastic, but was not her situation similar to that in millions of homes in our land? Is not this, basically, the reason why hundreds of thousands of our young people are looking for "thrills," for excitement, and turning to dope, crime, hoodlumism? There are other reasons, but they are subsidiary reasons really, for all reasons lead back to the home. In the home from which juvenile crime stems we usually discover either a state of anarchy prevailing because the home is without a head—due to divorce, drinking or mere abdication in favor of business—or we find a home where the sense of adventure is dead for another reason: because love is dead. Why did not the girl feel free to discuss with her parents what she felt about the way she lived? Why did she not feel that life itself was worth living? Perhaps the fact that she seldom saw her father and her mother except around the TV set is one reason. Accepting her description as accurate, she was living in a house filled with strangers who were not "present" to her, people between whom apparently flowed no communication of loving care or even interest in one another.

As Christians we know the whole message of Christ to be summed up in one word: Love. To be a Christian means to love. What the girl was hungry for—what she knew only as a great lack, a boredom—was love. What all the sad faces at the stoplights, all the hypochondriacs in the doctor's offices, all the steady drinkers near the bar are in need of is love. If our homes are not centers of Christian love, how can we expect our society to know the effects of that love? As the fathers of families we must be lovers. We must will the good of all those under our care. We must seek constantly for their perfection, recognizing that they, even the tiniest infants, have an absolute equality with us as persons. Our authority as rulers in our homes must always be used to achieve the highest possible good for those under our care. We do not use our authority for our own good—such is, indeed, the basic misuse—but for the temporal and eternal good which we will for those we love. The man who does not see his authority as essentially a means whereby he serves those under his rule neither knows what authority is nor deserves to have it. "To rule is to serve." But the service of the father is a service rooted in his love which will show itself in his constant effort to help to perfection those under his care.

The love of a man for his wife is a profound commitment to her good. That love is limitless the father soon discovers as it opens outward to the children born of his love for his wife. The child must be recognized not merely as the incarnation of the mutual love of the parents, but as a person, a body-soul unity having an intellect and a will and a destiny which is greater than any mere symbolizing of their union. And this child in its earliest years will know only one thing: whether or not he is himself loved. He will not be capable of any concrete return of that love for months and yet from his first hours he craves the knowledge of love. This knowledge, which flows into the baby's consciousness with the very milk it drinks, the air it breathes, the way it is handled, is crucial to the infant. More and more doctors and psychiatrists are insisting upon the fact that the healthy child physically and mentally is the child secure in the love of its parents. Not the finest of medical attention can compensate for the child's lack of love.

The child's need for love makes itself known through its demands for attention. Attention is a sign of love. Attention is but another way of saying that the child wants you to let it be "present" for you. But the child's demands for attention will diminish as soon as it "proves" to its satisfaction that it is loved. Here is another case where "love drives out fear," (I John 4:18) for the child's first thrusting out into the world is a traumatic experience and only a solid cushion of love can counteract the shock. That the child's overt demands for attention diminish should not mean that we pay less attention to it, that we cease to let it be "present" for us, or we "present" for it. The child has need of the loving, attentive father for all the years of his growth.

Attention. Both the advertising and entertainment industries are entirely devoted to the pursuit and capture of our attention. Each day we enter a world full of the confused noise and colors of those frantically clamoring for our attention in order to sell us something. This constant din of the professional attention-getters defeats its own purpose; unable to pay attention to all at once, most modern men have ceased to pay attention to any. We have, of necessity, become callous to even the most blatant sales appeals. To do otherwise would drive us mad. Even in those areas where attention is required of us, it has become exceedingly difficult. Magazine articles are sandwiched between advertisements; classroom lectures are interrupted by the sound of jets overhead; heavy traffic is made the more dangerous by highway billboards or neon signs. It is made more and more difficult for us to give our undivided attention even when we wish to do so. Yet, one of the ways in which we evidence our love for others is by paying attention to them, by allowing them to be "present" for us.

A human being in need of us, if only as listeners, does not announce that need in neon lights, does not dramatize that need through the medium of an eye-catching advertisement or through the breathless voice of an announcer. Some human beings have, indeed, been driven to extremities in order to focus our attention on their plight: the man who slashed his wrists was one such, and even that failed him. But most struggle to maintain a surface calm even when they are inwardly agonizing. "Those who are unhappy have no need for anything in this world," Simone Weil wrote, "but people capable of giving them their attention." In order to give others this attention which is their greatest need, we must look upon them not as "wife," "child," "patient," "business acquaintance," but as "myself." That this is difficult no one denies. Simone Weil calls it a "miracle," but if it is a "miracle," it is a miracle of grace. Christ who commanded us to do it will not withhold from us the graces necessary to the fulfillment of his command.

We ought, however, to be careful of mistaking a sentry-like watching for this attentiveness, especially in the case of our children. To be overly conscious of everything the child does, to be ever fearful of the infant's every move, always on the watch to warn and interrupt, is to render the child totally insecure. Such a persistent hounding is the farthest thing from true attentiveness that can be imagined and it can do untold psychological damage to the child. No, true attentiveness is that which allows the child to be present as he is at the moment, to accept him and love him for what he is and through that acceptance and love to provide him the security in which he can grow free from fear or nagging harassment.

"Fear not for I am with you . . ." "Do not be afraid . . ." How often these words appear in Sacred Scripture. It was into a frightened and utterly hopeless world that Christ was born. Love came to drive out fear and hatred and violence. It is significant to note how many of His miracles involved some personal contact between Him and the person on whom the miracle was performed: the blind man felt the Lord's fingers apply the moistened earth, the sick felt the touch of His hand. Everywhere His love was expressed in that sort of personal relationship, a very human relationship. His apostles and disciples whom He loved went out without fear or hatred and told others about Him. They had no guns or bombs, no TV's, microphones or rotary presses; the world was not changed by such things as these, but by the love these men had for Christ and for their fellow men. It was a personal love that they preached—and it is a personal love that we are called upon to practice.

But Christ commanded more than just the love of our neighbors: "But I tell you, Love your enemies, do good to those who hate you, pray for those who persecute and insult you, that so you may be true sons of your Father in heaven. . . . If you love those who love you, what title have you to a reward? Will not the publicans do as much? If you greet none but your brethren, what are you doing more than others? Will not the very heathen do as much? But you are to be perfect, as your heavenly Father is perfect." (Matt. 5:44, 46-48)

It is easy to love our neighbor, even our enemy, in the abstract, but it becomes more difficult when he lives with us. What is our child when he is interfering with our talk, tearing up our magazines or racing through the front room but the particular little "enemy" we are called upon to love at that moment? If our love is not to stop within the confines of our home, or even at the periphery of our circle of friends, it must yet begin at home. How can we expect to love those who hate us if we do not know even how to love those who live under our very roofs and who love us? On the other hand, love, once we have recognized it and disciplined ourselves to its practice, will diffuse itself; it cannot be contained. The man who has learned to love his children when they are his "enemies" has made the first step towards loving strangers who are his enemies.

That love calls for the sacrifice of self should come as no surprise. The essence of love is sacrifice. We have the constant reminder of the Cross that it is through sacrifice that love is proved. "God has proved his love to us by laying down his life for our sakes;" St. John tells us: "we too must be ready to lay down our lives for the sake of our brethren." (I John 3:16) No love worthy of the name can stop at words, it will express itself in action. If to love is to will the good of the other, then the ultimate in love is to offer up the greatest good we ourselves possess, our own lives, for the good of the other. Let us not make the mistake of thinking that this offering up of our lives must take the form of a martyrdom on the battlefield or a heroic moment during a shipwreck; it is a sacrifice that we who are married have already made. At the time of our wedding we gave up our lives for the good of the one we loved. Our heroic moments occur every day—whenever we have to deny ourselves for others. The lifelong sacrifice of ourselves to the good of others is what constitutes our paternity in its fullness. It would be worthwhile for us to examine our consciences regularly to see whether or not we are fulfilling that first promise. How often lately have we taken back the gift of ourselves which we offered before the altar of God? If we have allowed "business" and the world to make us forget it, we have called back the sacrifice, we have recanted at the stake. What was meant to be our martyrdom and our triumph has become our treason and our defeat.

It is hard to love even when that love is returned. Even the best will in the world cannot, at times, overcome all fatigue, cannot restrain the momentary sharpness of the tongue or the quickness to respond to one hurt by another. The ego when hurt would sulk, licking its wounds and snapping at those who approach. Pride will rear its head angrily, humiliation will desire the luxury of self-pity.

Failure will seek a scapegoat upon whom the guilt can be lashed. More often than not, the wounded ego, the stung pride, the sense of failure will be due to some event that occurred outside of the home, at the job or in the course of the day's activities and the temptation will be strong to bring these hurts home, to make others suffer for what we have suffered. To assent to this is to open the gates of the family to the enemy of love. When our love is not returned, or is not returned in the way we think that it should be, the temptation is even stronger. At such times we must remember that the call to love is not a call conditioned by any expectation of return. Our love for others is to be patterned after the love of Him who "gave us his love first." (I John 4:19) And the pattern of Christ's love is the Cross, the humiliation, the agony, the death which He suffered for our sake. The Cross, sign of failure for the non-believer, is for the Christian the sign of love. Christ, the Bridegroom, gave life to His Bride, the Church, by His death on the Cross.

The father cannot expect either his marriage or his family to survive if he forgets that his greatest obligation is one which he shares with all Christians: the obligation to love. To the degree that he loves without thought of return, to the extent that he looks upon even his enemy as infinitely precious in the sight of God and therefore infinitely worthy of his own attention and care, he is loving that person, however weakly, as God loves him. When his love for another leads him to the exchange of the vows of Holy Matrimony, then his love is caught up into the supernatural, he truly gives and receives a love transfigured by the love of Christ. United in the love of Christ, husband and wife, living in the sacrament, loving in the sacrament, will find that their sacrificial love like all true sacrifice will be rendered fruitful by God: it will bear new life. Having given up their lives in Christ, they will have life more fully. "It is the man who loses his life for my sake that will secure it." (Matt. 16:25) God may grant the couple the grace of children, that they might more readily see that love *is* life, but should He withhold this blessing their marriage will yet be fruitful. Their shared love in Christ becomes a shared life in Christ, the means to their mutual sanctification, the preparation for that ultimate life with God Who is Love.

Chapter III

THE FATHER AS CHRIST

"This love is an eminently human one since it is directed from one person to another through an affection of the will; it involves the good of the whole person, and therefore can enrich the expressions of body and mind with a unique dignity, ennobling these expressions as special ingredients and signs of the friendship distinctive of marriage. This love God has judged worthy of special gifts, healing, perfecting and exalting gifts of grace and of charity. Such love, merging the human with the divine, leads the spouses to a free and mutual gift of themselves, a gift providing itself by gentle affection and by deed; such love pervades the whole of their lives: indeed by its busy generosity it grows better and grows greater. Therefore it far excels mere erotic inclination, which, selfishly pursued, soon enough fades wretchedly away."

(Church in the modern world, No. 49).

"Christian spouses, in virtue of the sacrament of Matrimony, . . . signify and partake of the mystery of that unity and fruitful love which exists between Christ and His Church."

(Dogmatic constitution on the Church, No. 11).

We Tried in the last chapter to tell why love is not just a matter of the emotions and the senses. The extreme of looking upon man as merely an animal—which is the mistake of the sensualists—has its antipode in that error which denies the body, and which some have labeled "angelism."

Both extremes are the result of thinking of man as a two story building, the top floor being his "spiritual half" and the bottom floor being his "physical half." Some want to live in the upstairs and ignore the downstairs; more seem to live in the downstairs without realizing that there is an upstairs. Others would live in the elevator and spend their lives going up or down as the momentary occasion seems to warrant.

The whole notion is fostered and strengthened by those preachers and writers who, as much because of the limitations of language as for any reason, find it expedient to make clear and swift distinctions between man's "higher" and "lower" natures, his "spiritual" and "animal" self, his "lofty" or "base" motives, and so on. Too sharp a dichotomy is made between man's body and his soul; the soul, we are often warned, should dominate the body else the "bestial part" of man will rise up and tear him to pieces. Such warnings are full of truth, but they tend to leave one with the impression that God gave us a beautiful second story apartment to live in but for some odd and unexplained reason put underneath it a downstairs full of dark, unhealthy and menacing animals called "instincts," "drives" and "appetites," all of which are wicked and will devour us.

This is tragic, this thinking of oneself as a two story building; it is tragic because it does not conform to reality. Having notions of things which do not conform to the reality of things as God made them is the hothouse of anxieties, neuroses and mental illness. The unfortunate man who thinks of himself as a soul living on top of a body which is somehow unclean of its very nature is likely to find life as it is lived rather miserable. Marriage, since rooted in sex, will cause him the deepest mental distress for he must express the highest feelings of his soul through his body.

The Catholic, however should know that man is not a two story building, that he does not have two natures, animal and spiritual, but one human nature. He is indeed made up of matter and spirit, but he is not a soul living on top of a body; he is a body-soul unity. We can speak of the soul (the intelligence and free will) as "higher" than the body in the sense that it is the soul that is the image of God, but we should not conclude from this that the body is to be despised. Only the soul united with a body makes up a human person. The wound done to man by Original Sin was not done to his body alone, nor to his soul alone, but to man as a body-soul unity. The disorder we personally experience in ourselves as the result of that wound is as often a matter of the soul—the will failing to respond to the intellect—as it is of the body— the senses thrusting aside the dictates of reason. The Catholic knows, too, that even as the Church upholds the immortality of the soul, it defends at every point the high dignity of the body. The fact of the Incarnation and the doctrine of the Resurrection should alone give pause to those who think of the body of man as somehow ignoble.

Now the call to love another person within the sacrament of matrimony is a call to love that person not only with the good will we ought to show towards all, but also sexually. In marriage a man is called upon to love a woman in his totality, with his soul and his body. Marriage is neither the coming together of two souls or of two bodies, but of two persons. Their union is really a comm-union, a unique oneness of body and soul, and this oneness of husband and wife was willed by God from the beginning.

But why, throughout all of nature from the pistils and stamens of plants to the male and female of insects, birds, animals and men, did God introduce sexuality? We know that an act of the Divine Will accomplished this, but why? Since the image of the Creator is in all that He has created, and since sexuality is one of the most vibrant chords resounding throughout creation, God must find in sexuality something beautiful and truly expressive of Himself and of His own inner nature. Earlier we sketched the way in which the human family mirrors, though weakly, the inner life of the Trinity. Can there be more meaning yet in conjugal love?

In the New Testament we find that our Lord insisted upon the inviolability of the marriage bond as the work of God and beyond the tampering hands of men. We know, too, that He elevated marriage to the supernatural level of a sacrament, crowning the natural institution of marriage with a supernatural glory. St. Paul, in the course of his Epistle to the Ephesians treats of the union of man and wife that is now a union in Christ. The passage for centuries used as the Epistle of the Nuptial Mass should be meditated upon regularly by the father of a family.

"Wives must obey their husbands as they would obey the Lord." (Ephes. 5:22) The word "obey" sounds harsh to us. Perhaps it conjures up the picture of the absolute patriarch of pagan times whose wife was little more than a slave and who, along with her children, was under the absolute rule of the father. We remember from our history that the power of life and death was in his hands and that he exercised it, though most often in regard to new unwanted children, who were commonly allowed to die by exposure to elements and animals. The thought revolts us. We want love, not obedience. Even that obedience—which is a mixture of love and respect (and perhaps fear?)

—which we expect from our children, we do not desire from the woman we love.

Such thinking about this command is not uncommon, but it misses the point. If we read further, we find, "The man is the head to which the woman's body is united, just as Christ is the head of the Church, he, the Saviour on whom the safety of his body depends; and women must owe obedience at all points to their husbands, as the Church does to Christ." (Ephes. 5:23-24)

The obedience of the wife then is not grounded in fear, or in any mixture of love and fear, but flows from her very relationship with her husband. The immediate significance of her subjection to him is grounded on the natural hierarchy of the family. The husband has the responsibility of guarding and caring for his wife; she is dependent upon him. The ultimate meaning of the wife's obedience and the husband's headship is that the marriage of man and wife images the eternal union of Christ and His Church. Wifely obedience is none other than wifely love, which is wifely in that it submits. More than the desire to please her husband, this submissiveness is a realization of a woman's desire to rest secure in the strength of her husband, to have him rule and guide the household, to leave to him the really grave decisions. A woman who can so rely upon her husband is a woman liberated from a man's responsibilities and freed to be more fully a wife. Indeed, if a woman does not know this submissiveness then she is not aware of wifely love. She remains unfulfilled as a woman and her husband, for want of a wife's love, will remain stunted in his growth as a man. Within marriage, his maturity is meant to come through the realization of his wife's dependence upon his headship. Only if her love is the obedience-love of a wife can her husband give her the love of a husband which is the love Christ has for His Church.

All the responsibility, however, is not the wife's; the husband must provide the atmosphere in which she will flower, in which her submission comes naturally to her as she becomes more woman and wife. If all the love-giving is on her side, the husband could easily become an exacting tyrant, and tyranny breeds rebellion. "You who are husbands must shew love to your wives, as Christ shewed love to the Church when he gave himself up on its behalf." (Ephes. 5:25) If the wife manifests her love in obedience, how does the husband show his love? By being Christ-like in his self-sacrifice. The love of husband for wife is meant to be so unhesitatingly selfless that it will not stop short of the complete sacrifice of life itself for the good of the beloved, even as Christ died on the cross for His Bride. Few of us, however, are asked to actually die for those we love; what is normally required of us is patience, generosity, good humor, an awareness of the needs of our wives and a willingness to meet those needs. To show love to our wives is to provide them with all the assurances of word and gesture which are so necessary to their full awakening as wives. The wife depends upon the husband, is submissive to him; he has the obligation of being dependable and full of care for her.

Material care is far less important to a woman than the knowledge that she is loved, wanted, needed by her husband. Only in the security of the knowledge that she is loved can she give totally of herself. The husband who has allowed his love-demonstrations to become a matter of an occasional "romantic" moment, or has let his love-making become a bedroom routine, or has allowed the very thought of love-signs to wither away as the years have gone by, has removed from his wife the very air upon which her fulfillment as a wife depends for its life. More, he has stunted his own growth as a man. His maturity was meant to come through his realization and acceptance of his wife's dependence upon his leadership. In neglecting to help her to flower into full womanhood, he has lost his opportunity to become more manly. Our land is full of men and women so unfulfilled: women unsure of being wanted, needed or loved turning to hypochondria, alcohol, or to the children, jobs, club activities, not to mention other men, for that assurance; men seeking various ways from flirtations, light affairs, to adultery to prove their masculinity. Even when the high fires of the wedding day do not reduce to the burnt charcoal of the divorce courtroom, the radiance has been allowed to die out. What was a mutual desire to give, an outward flow of the self to the other, has become only a desire to receive, a grasping after personal warmth that masquerades as love. The intimacy of marriage has become not the source of mutual enrichment, but of mutual impoverishment.

This need not be so; indeed, it is so only because men and women have permitted their love to become in a sense sacrilegious. They have reduced a sacred and holy relationship, a relationship which mirrors that of Christ and His Church, to the level of the profane. They have ignored the life of God which flows through their marriage, they have denied the life of God in their partners.

We should remind ourselves often that the person we have married has a redeemed body, a redeemed soul, that within her in a most personal way dwells the Triune God, that she has a life in God and that we have an obligation through our marriage vows to do what we can to foster that life. We should remember to thank God for the gift of this woman, to ask His blessing upon her, His graces that we might be worthy of the calling he has given us. The "I love you" whispered to her should be a benediction: "May you be richly blessed." "May you reach heaven." St. Paul applies to the head of the family the following words about the relationship of Christ and His Church: "He would hallow it, purify it by bathing it in the water to which his word gave life; he would summon it into his own presence, the Church in all its beauty, no stain, no wrinkle, no such disfigurement; it was to be holy, it was to be spotless." (Ephes. 5:26-27)

Holiness is the high purpose of wifely obedience, then; the stewardship of holiness is the responsibility of the head. Through her submissiveness to her husband, her union with him, the wife is to be revealed in all her beauty, to grow in purity and holiness. By helping her to be the person God wants her to be, by liberating in her the personality uniquely her own—the personality which he and perhaps only he among men knows and loves—he is helping her to sanctity. Was it not that vision of her uniqueness that overwhelmed him; was this not what he "saw" that others did not see? The husband who takes every care to safeguard and protect his wife, who leaves no moral stain upon her by his lack of consideration, no psychological disfigurement to come about through his selfishness, will find that his marriage will be a continuously richer experience as the years advance. As husband and wife grow closer to God, they are themselves more closely united.

"And that is how husband ought to love wife," St. Paul continues, "as if she were his own body; in loving his wife, a man is but loving himself." (Ephes. 5:28)

Earlier we caught a glimpse of what loving others as we love ourselves means; here, St. Paul repeats the command of Christ but adds to it a particular emphasis: the married man is truly loving himself when he shows love to his wife, for she is bound to him not only by the spirit but also by the strongest of all fleshly ties. "It is unheard of, that a man should bear ill-will to his own flesh and blood; no, he keeps it fed and warmed; and so it is with Christ and his Church; we are limbs of his body; flesh and bone, we belong to him." (Ephes. 5:29-30)

Through our baptism we are incorporated into Christ and through that union with Christ we participate in the very life of God as it flows unceasingly from the Head to the Body of the Church. The early Church was full of the realization of the immensity, the almost unbearable greatness of this divine adoption. "See how the Father has shewn his love towards us"; St. John calls out, his words almost breaking under his wonder and joy, "that we should be counted as God's sons, should be his sons." (I John 3:1) If we are sons of the Father, it is because we "have put on the person of Christ." (Gal. 3:27) Like water

mixed with wine, we have come, as the liturgy of the
Eucharist says, "to share in the divinity of Christ, who
humbled himself to share in our humanity." All that we
do is done "Through Him, with Him, in Him."

This oneness of Christ and His Church, of Christ and
the Christians who are "limbs of his body," is the reality
which our marriages image. When two who "belong to
him" come together before His altar, the place of sacrifice,
to make the sacrifice of themselves, they are no longer two
but one. They have been called not only to the union
which God instituted as a foreshadowing of the marriage
of Divinity and humanity which was the Incarnation, but
also as St. Paul explains, to image the extension of that
mystery, the union of the Eternal Bridegroom with His
Spouse.

But we are limited creatures and truly perfect unity in
marriage we cannot expect. Personalities are not obliter-
ated at the altar and adjustments must be made by each
party. The very differences between man and woman
which attracted them to each other may become the
source of difficulties after marriage, but in seeking unity
with one another they shall find happiness, pleasure, joy
and that wholeness of a mature marriage. Ill-will arises
when either party is seeking not unity but something for
the self, the gratification of some personal desire. Ill-will
is destructive of unity; it is the root of isolation. The man
who bears ill-will cannot claim to love, for to love is to
will good. And the man who does not love is a man
isolated, a man who will never find unity, for in order to
know those fleeting moments of rapture that dazzle the
consciousness with their beauty, there must be a surrender
of the self, a full giving in love. The fragmentary glimpses
of that beatific vision granted to man and wife are gained,
even as the Beatific Vision itself is gained, through love.

But if a man should not bear ill-will to his own flesh
and blood, it is not solely because they are his flesh and
blood, but because they are Christ's. The caresses husband
and wife exchange are caresses given to Christ. The flesh

touched with the fingertips is flesh that belongs to Christ, that is surrendered in Christ. And the fingers that touch are meant to be Christ's, too, and the love they express is meant to be a sanctifying love.

The more perfectly the husband identifies his headship of the family with the headship of Christ, the more he strives to pattern himself and his giving after Christ, the more perfectly will his marriage image the union of Christ and His Church. "That is why a man will leave his father and mother and cling to his wife, and the two will become one flesh. Yes, those words are a high mystery, and I am applying them here to Christ and his Church." (Ephes. 5:31-32)

Is there any mystery more difficult to penetrate than that of the union of Christ and His Church, a real, supernatural union of Christ and each individual Christian that binds all into a oneness? For St. Paul it was *the* mystery of the Gospels; all else flows from it, including the Redemption. And here, St. Paul tells us explicitly that this mystery is intimately related to the mystery of the sacrament of marriage. By quoting the Old Testament, St. Paul reminds us that matrimony was divinely ordained from the beginning; in applying those words to Christ and His Church, he unveils for us that the matrimonial union between a Christian man and a Christian woman is a symbolizing of the union of Christ and His Church. As there is but one Bride, the Church, and one Bridegroom, Christ, so the marriage bond unites one man and one woman. Theirs is a total commitment until death. Our Lord underscored not only this unity but also its indissolubility when he said "what God, then, has joined, let not man put asunder." (Matt. 19:6) Just as man cannot sunder the union of God and man in Christ, just as man cannot tear the Head from the body of the Church, divorce the Bridegroom from His one true Bride, neither can man dissolve that oneness of man and wife.

Moreover, the union of Christ and His Church has as its purpose the birth of men into the God-life of sanctifying grace. The marriage union has as its purpose the birth of men into this natural life that they might be "born again" into the supernatural life of grace. The seed of the husband flowing into the womb of the wife to generate new life was seen by the early Greek fathers as a symbol of the grace of Christ flowing into His Bride, the Church, to generate saints. This symbolizing is the living out of the sanctity specific to marriage. In the marital union the making of sexual love is the outward signing which, working with God, is the communicating of grace by the spouses to one another; it is an encounter with Christ who is present and active in a very special way during this dynamic union which is a living realization of His own supernatural life-giving union with His Church.

The first gift of husband and wife to each other is the gift of sacramental sanctifying grace—the gift of Life, of that abundant life which Christ brought to us. "I have come so that they may have life, and have it more abundantly." (John 10:10). Throughout their conjugal life, in all their attempts to make one another happy, in the marriage act and in all their shared experiences, joyous and heart-breaking, they will continue to be for one another the instruments of divine life. Every grace conferred upon man or wife, including those from the other sacraments, will be a grace to perfect them further and to help them fulfill their high and difficult vocation of faithfully imaging Christ's own nuptials.

The headship of the husband becomes the headship of the father when God chooses to give the man and wife a concrete manifestation of the invisible life which flows through their union through the birth of children. And it is not surprising that St. Paul, immediately after treating of the relationship of husband and wife, turns to a consideration of the relationship of parent and child. "You who are children must shew obedience in the Lord to your parents; it is your duty; Honour thy father and thy mother —that is the first commandment which has a promise attached to it—so it shall go well with thee, and thou shalt live long to enjoy the land." (Ephes. 6:1-3) Yet none of us does well to invoke this commandment without pondering the lines which follow it and complete it: "You who are fathers, do not rouse your children to resentment; the training, the discipline in which you bring them up must come from the Lord." (Ephes. 6:4)

"From the Lord." "In the Lord." All members of a family are equal before God, all are unique and sacred personalities destined for the same Beatific Vision. The natural hierarchy of authority in the family is protected from abuse by those words "From the Lord." It is not for himself that the father rules, but as the minister of Christ. Not only can he not command anything contrary to Christian law, but also he must see to it that those subject to his rule are formed in Christ, through a discipline rooted in love. Surely that father who punishes a child more severely than the misdemeanor merits is failing to discipline as the Lord would discipline. The tyrannical parent, the selfish or unfair parent—and how quickly children recognize unfairness—is the one who rouses his child to resentment and rebellion. Such fathers are, however, probably more rare than those who are overindulgent, who refuse to chastise their children at all. This lack of correction, usually stemming from sentimentality, often disguises itself as love. These rouse their children to resentment, too, the resentment the child feels at not having the order and serenity which only authority can impose and which the child subconsciously craves. In addition, both the tyrannical and the overindulgent parent rouse in the child a resentment of any later attempt to impose discipline or authority upon him.

"Spare the rod," the Old Testament tells us, "and thou art no friend to thy son; ever a kind father is quick to punish." (Prov. 13:24) Does it sound strange that we should be told that it is the kind father who is quick to punish, that the man who exercises his authority is the friend to his son? Yet any gardener knows that a beautiful flower or a healthy hedge is the result of pruning dead or wayward shoots. The undisciplined shrub, the unpruned rose bush are both soon ugly. The father who loves his children—who wills their good—will not let them grow up without direction, training and discipline. To do otherwise is to deprive them of that promise attached to their observance of the fourth commandment: "So it shall go well with thee, and thou shalt live long to enjoy the land." Nearly all of our "problem children," our juvenile delinquents, all of those children with whom things have not gone well and who are not living to "enjoy the land," come from homes lacking a head.

Christianity's revolutionary truth about marriage has been under attack in recent centuries. The rupture of Christendom, and the secularization of society which rapidly followed, have dragged many back to a life lived by pagan standards. Divorce, unknown in the early ages of Christianity, is now present as a possibility for all. The pagan practices of polygamy and polyandry, with only slight alteration—the husbands and wives are successive instead of simultaneous—are with us again. Abortion, differing from the pagan method of exposure only by the fact that it occurs earlier, is on the increase. Sterilization, allowing for the pursuit of sexual gratification without responsibility, is as common today as it was uncommon a generation ago. The ancient sin of Onan, whereby he "frustrated the act of marriage" (Gen. 38:9) has been refined by modern medical technology and is today hailed a boon to mankind. Some non-Catholic religious leaders, rejecting both the natural law and the sacramentality of marriage, even publicly urge Onan's crime upon us. Finally, sex is deified again as it was by the pagans. The current fixation on women's breasts is not too far from the pagan phallic worship. The pagan cults, however, reverenced sex as a mystery, the mystery of fertility, while contemporary entertainment, advertisements, mass publications and "marriage manuals" see it only as a sort of toy. Ironically enough, this return to a world of pseudo-paganism, this rejection of the new and return to the old, is thought by a huge number of our fellow men to be "progress."

One of the more important factors behind this return to false paganism has been the decline of the sense of the sacred among men, the loss of that awareness of God's reflection in all that He has created. The popular deification of science, most common among non-scientists, has stunted in the souls of many the sense of mystery, of awe and reverence before the wonders of God. "As you stand in awe of Christ," St. Paul says, "submit to each other's rights." (Ephes. 5:21) But if "awe of Christ" diminishes?

Basically, the disintegration of the family has kept pace with the loss of Christ-consciousness in men. It is "as Christ" that the father rules in the home, it is as "His Church" that women hold their proper place of love and respect there. With the secularization of society that flowed out of the sundering of Christendom, men have had the consciousness of their oneness with Christ all but washed from their minds. The first "reformers" slashed away at man's Church consciousness. But Christ and His Church are one and it was inevitable that with the loss of Church consciousness men should lose their consciousness of Christ.

The effect of this on the family was immediate, for it is only in full awareness of their union with Christ that men can adequately fulfill their roles as the heads of families. If men no longer look upon themselves as united with Christ, as taking Christ's place in the home, as assuming the specific role of Christ in the symbolic drama that is marriage, then how can they possibly look upon their wives as Brides of Christ, as the Church of Christ? And if they do not see this, what basis is there for a wife's obedience to her husband, for a husband's self-sacrifice and tender dedication to his wife? The man who recognizes that what goes on in marriage is nothing more or less than what goes on between Christ and His Church can see the pattern he is to follow, can understand the meaning of unity, indissolubility, love, protection, fruitfulness, obedience and sanctity as they exist in marriage. But what about the man who is insensible to Christ or to His Church?

Couples having the highest of ideals, but lacking the life that flows through the marriage that is a sacrament cannot be more to each other than each one is. If the marriage ever demands more than this? Who can guarantee himself that it never will? Is it to avoid crises too severe for their unaided love that such couples often avoid children—or too many children? And what about couples who do not have the highest of ideals? The unity they think they have found in the pleasure of sex may endure for a while, but the sum of human experience tells us that this is a false unity and that all attempts to found unity on sexual desire alone are doomed. Desire is not love. Desire seeks to get not to give and a marriage based on desire rather than love is soon clawed to shreds by a mutual grasping.

The return to paganism which we see as a result of the loss of Christ-consciousness is not a return to the paganism of the pre-Christian West, however much appearances may seem to proclaim it. A de-Christianized society is of necessity inferior to the pagan civilization which preceded it. One reason for this is that all the good in paganism was "baptized," caught up and brought into the service of Christ. Thus, the home today that has not the headship of Christ lacks too the headship of the pagan patriarch. It lacks all headship whatsoever.

Christians are not alone in deploring the disintegration of family life that has followed the flood of neopaganism. Writers steeped in secularism and journals born from it have for years been seeking ways to restore life to those unhappy homes which are the chief victims of moral erosion and are now the source of so many of our social ills. Valiant as some of these endeavors might be, most, if not all, of them are condemned to failure because they treat only the symptoms and do not attack the disease itself. Some do hint at the spiritual roots of the illness when they advise families to attend church together, but more often than not this advice stems from the erroneous notion that religion is meant to serve man rather than to be man's way of worshipping God. To advise religion as one might advise a pill is to make banal the highest activity of man. God is "the beginning of all things and their end," (Apoc. 22: 13) and to treat Him as a psychological or social prop is to mock Him.

Most popular writers, however, offer solutions to the problems posed by family disintegration from which God is altogether excluded. Some talk of the family as a "team" to be ruled by democratic procedure and see a stronger home life issuing from a voting arrangement whereby all members of the family will have a voice in important family decisions. Others, more business than politically minded, speak of husband and wife treating their marriage as a business partnership; extreme forms of this advise separate bank accounts, etc., while milder forms call for all important decisions to be the result of the full agreement of both parties. More recently, some have heralded "togetherness" as the answer to the problem. Recreation as a family group is seen by the advocates of "togetherness" as the source of greater family unity.

None of these solutions is totally wrong; what is wrong is that they are considered solutions. Some family problems can, indeed, be worked out best by common arrangement or discussion among the more mature members of the family. Democratic procedure, however, if it is not to be carried to absurd extremes, must be controlled and have its limits when one is dealing with children. Even if parents were willing—and there seems no mass movement to this sort of thing—there are numerous decisions which children are totally unqualified to make and which parents must make themselves.

Actually, the partnership idea of shared headship is the more popular notion today. Modern living has blurred the distinction between masculine and feminine labors and privileges as never before. Our grandfathers would no more have thought of doing the baby's diapers than our grandmothers would have considered smoking a cigarette in a bar. There is a greater degree of collaboration between man and wife in business, social and political affairs than at any time in the past. This increased intimacy has its value in that it binds husband and wife closer together in their mutual task. It can bear the beautiful fruit of that consideration asked by the Apostles of husbands for their wives. However, it can also blur the fundamental distinction between the functions of man and wife, which it surely does when the wife with her own income, her own car, her own bank account, can come to consider herself a free agent independent of her husband. Moreover, most women unconsciously, if not consciously, resent being treated as business-partners by the men they love. Something deep within feminine nature needs the strength and decisive leadership of a manly husband. Even if the sense of independence does no damage, even if the feminine desire for submission does not bring difficulties, the partnership arrangement holds yet other troubles in store. If both parties do not agree when there is a real difference of opinion—about the husband's changing jobs, for instance—then the decision must either be left unmade and the opportunity lost, or the job undertaken against the wife's wishes. Either choice sows the seeds of discord.

Those who see "togetherness" as the spring of family unity do not seem to understand that, fine as recreational pursuits undertaken as a family may be, they are the result of and not the cause of a unified family.

Such timid and shallow panaceas as these do damage even in homes where they are not accepted, for they ignore and by implication deny the Christian teaching about family headship and thus weaken the position of that father who is striving to meet the obligations of his calling. Other corrosive agents are at work, too: the many television and radio programs, movies and comic strips, where the father is the butt of all jokes, the moron who must be protected from himself or patiently endured by wife and children. If the notion of the headship of the family is an impoverished one, emptied of meaning for many, that is but a testimonial to the degree of damage already done by the secular atmosphere in which we live. Perhaps it might be worthwhile for us the next time we see "father" being made the boob of the story to compare the role of this "father" with the high dignity and rich meaning of Christian paternity. Renewal can come, for men and families, only through Christ who said, "Behold, I make all things new." (Apoc. 21:5) Only when we fathers become aware of the "high and treasured promises" (II Peter 1:4) bestowed on us, that we are sharers in the divine nature, only when we see that our marriage is meant to reflect the glorious splendor of that marriage which is the archetype and foundation of all true marriages, only then will the water of our marriages be, as at Cana, changed to wine by the love of Christ. Then we will have set our feet on the path that leads to "the wedding-feast of the Lamb." (Apoc. 19:7)

Chapter IV

THE FATHER AS PRIEST

"The training for the apostolate should start with the children's earliest education. In a special way however, adolescents and young persons should be initiated into the apostolate and imbued with its spirit. This formation must be perfected throughout their whole life in keeping with the demands of new responsibilities. It is evident, therefore, that those who have the obligation to provide a Christian education also have the duty of providing formation for the apostolate. In the family parents have the task of training their children from childhood on to recognize God's love for all men. By example especially they should teach them little by little to be solicitous for the material and spiritual needs of their neighbour. The whole family in its common life, then, should be a sort of apprenticeship for the apostolate. Children must be educated, too, in such fashion that transcending the family circle, they may open their minds to both ecclesiastical and temporal communities. They should be so involved in the local community of the parish that they will acquire a consciousness of being living and active members of the people of God."

(*Apostolate of the Laity*, No. 30).

IN ONE of the earliest centuries of the Church, St. John Chrysostom called the Christian home an *ecclesia domestica,* a "family church." The truth borne in this statement is easily grasped upon a moment's reflection.

There have been times and places, there are today countries in the world, where the Church is kept alive only in the home, where—with priests imprisoned or executed and any public manifestation of religion forbidden —the only sacraments possible are those of baptism and marriage and the entire religious life of the family can only be carried on in the hidden recesses of the home. In such a situation the father of a family cannot escape knowing the profound responsibility and the true dignity, the priestly dignity, of his fatherhood.

We Americans lack the grace of such hardship—and such hardship is a grace if it leads us closer to God. It is easier for us to lose sight of the responsibilities which the father shares in common with a priest of the Church, manifold responsibilities as teacher and caretaker of souls. If we may call an ordained priest "father" and by that refer to his true if not actual paternal relationship to those under his care, we may call the father "priest" and by that refer to his role as teacher of doctrine and morality and as leader of that spiritual community which is his family.

But there is a further and deeper meaning hidden in St. John Chrysostom's definition of the home as a "family church," and a deeper meaning, too, in our identification of the father as a "priest." St. Paul's teaching on marriage clearly states that the father's authority in the home is an authority to be respected because it comes from Christ. St. Paul could advise wives: "Let women be subject to their husbands as to the Lord." (Eph. 5:22) Every Christian is another Christ, but the father of a family shares in the priestly dignity of Christ in a special way.

Through the sacraments of baptism and confirmation all Christians share in the priesthood of Christ the High Priest. "You were made a priest at baptism," St. John Chrysostom says. His words were echoed by Pope Pius XII who pointed out that while the priest and the priest alone as the representative of Christ has the power to consecrate the bread and wine, it is by virtue of their lay priesthood that the faithful can join with the priest in offering the Divine Victim. "Nor is it to be wondered at," his holiness writes in *Mediator Dei*, "that the faithful should be raised to this dignity. By the waters of baptism, as by common right, Christians are made members of the Mystical Body of Christ the Priest, and by the 'character' which is imprinted on their souls, they are appointed to give worship to God. Thus, they participate, according to their condition, in the priesthood of Christ."

It is by and through their incorporation in the Body of Christ, their sharing in His priesthood, that two Christians are able to confer upon each other the sacrament of matrimony. It is wrong to say of some couple that "Father So and so married them," for he did not. They married each other and Father So and so was but the Church's witness at that moment when they conferred upon each other that sacrament which will unite them in a conjugal union that is an image of Christ's union with His Church. This is not to put the sacrament of matrimony outside the Church, or somehow (as the early Protestants did) to put undue emphasis on the priesthood of the laity, for both the priesthood of the laity and the sacrament of matrimony presuppose the Church and cannot exist without the Church.

A Christian life is a life focused on the Mass, one which is constantly refreshed and strengthened by this central act of Christian worship. The Mass is a corporate act of worship, a social act rather than a time for private devotions, and the family—as the basic social and liturgical body—should, if at all possible, participate in it together. A father and mother attending Mass with their children to offer thanks and to seek the graces necessary to keep their family one in charity, one in Christ, are performing their most important common act.

The worry of children being the cause of distraction is one that can be countered by a little advance preparation and common sense. First, the children should be imbued with a spirit of reverence for the Mass and for "God's house" before they are brought to Church. This is not something one does with a threat or two before entering the Church, but is an attitude fostered in all their prayer-times, their visits to the Church with one or the other of their parents during the week, and by the whole atmosphere at home. Children who realize that attendance at Mass is a privilege will seldom be a problem in Church or during Mass.

Even very young children—like our three year old—find the Mass itself fascinating. For the Mass is a drama, a liturgical drama clothed in richly embroidered vestments, surrounded by floral displays and candles. Even a child too young to understand much of what is taking place can find something to interest him. The father should simply call the wandering attention of one of his children back to the altar by pointing out that "Now the priest is washing his hands," or "Now the priest is pouring wine into the chalice. Soon he will change it into the blood of Jesus." Parents should do the reverse of what seems to be the custom and take their children up to the very front pew, where they can see what is going on. The distracting child at Mass is the bored child, the child frightened by a sea of strange hats or the child deserted in the midst of a strange group of people while one or the other of his parents is going to communion. If the parents sat in one of the front pews, the children, far from feeling frightened at the departure of either parent, could watch and learn as the father and mother received the Sacred Host.

Some might be shocked at the thought of teaching the children while at Mass. Yet historically the entire fore-mass, the mass of the catechumens, was just that—a time of instruction for those entering the Church. There is no reason why the father or mother should not whisper brief, pointed explanations to the children at various points of the Mass excluding, of course, the most solemn moment of Transubstantiation. In this the father is fulfilling one of the obligations of his lay-priesthood, the doctrinal instruction of his children in the most important of Christian acts.

The whole atmosphere at home is important in fostering in the children a proper attitude toward the Mass. The Mass should not be an isolated hour of worship in an otherwise secular week, but this is exactly what it will be to our children if that is what it is to us. If God is the supreme reality and the highest good in our lives, then this will make itself evident in our lives. The father who participates in the Mass regularly gives to his children a far more convincing statement as to the importance of the Mass than all his words do. "One of the greatest things my father ever did for me," a friend once said, "was to take me aside one evening and tell me that I was old enough to go to Mass with him every morning if I wished. If I wished . . . I wished nothing more. I'll never forget those silent walks to Church in the quiet hours of the morning and our kneeling together at the communion rail."

But if the principle act of Catholic worship is outside the home, within the home the liturgy has a place, too. By this time no father should be ignorant of the many

valuable pamphlets and books on the liturgy in the home.*
For the responsibility of a father is first and foremost to
provide that environment which will enable those holy
innocents under his care to flower into saints. Such an
environment is not produced by the purchasing of religious
objects for the home, but by the tone of the life lived
there.

As Americans we seem to have a natural impulse to
look for a technique that will give us in any particular
field the desired results. We want to know always what
we must do actively, in order to accomplish our ends.
In certain areas—building a house, flying an airplane, op-
erating a lathe—the matter of technique, knowing what
to do and when to do it, is crucial. But we must not allow
our American talent for technique to lead us astray when
we approach the realm of the spirit. In the religious
sphere it is not so much *doing* that counts, as it is *being*.
To do an act of charity without being charitable—giving
money to a beggar to get rid of him, or in order to let
others see how charitable we are—is not to do an act of
charity at all. In fact, such an act can be a sin of selfishness
or pride. To adorn the home with holy water fonts and
crucifixes or pictures of the saints is meaningless—and can
be a travesty—unless these things are an expression of the
life that is lived there.

And that life must be a life lived in Christ. The Mass
never ends. As the Council Fathers point out: "Christ
the Lord, High Priest taken from among men, 'made a
kingdom and priests to God his Father' (Apoc. 1:6; cf.
5:9-10) out of this new people. The baptized, by regen-

* A postcard request sent to the following addresses will bring
lists or catalogues of material related to the Christian Family:
The Abbey Press, St. Meinrad, Indiana 47577
The Family Life Division, United States Catholic
    Conference, 1312 Mass. Ave., N. W., Washington
    D. C. 20005
The Liturgical Press, St. John's Abbey, Collegeville,
    Minn. 56321

eration and the anointing of the Holy Spirit, are conse-
crated into a spiritual house and a holy priesthood. Thus,
through all those works befitting Christian men they can
offer spiritual sacrifices and proclaim the power of Him
who has called them out of darkness into His marvelous
light (cf. I Peter 2:4-10). Therefore all the disciples of
Christ, persevering in prayer and praising God (cf. Acts
2:42-47), should present themselves as living sacrifice,
holy and pleasing to God (cf. Rom. 12:1). Everywhere
on earth they must bear witness to Christ and give an
answer to those who seek an account of that hope of
eternal life which is in them (cf. I Peter 3:15)." (Dogmatic constitution on the Church; p. 10)

The father of a family "bears witness" in a number of
ways. Some we have already discussed, some will be mentioned in later chapters. Here we might fruitfully pause
to consider the fact that, in discussing the priesthood of
all the faithful, the Council Fathers took note of the fact
that "Christian spouses, in virtue of the sacrament of matrimony, signify and partake of the mystery of that unity
and fruitful love which exists between Christ and His
Church (cf. Eph. 5:32). The spouses thereby help each
other to attain to holiness in their married life and by
the rearing and education of their children. And so, in
their state and way of life, they have their own special
gift among the People of God (cf. I Cor. 7:7).

"For from the wedlock of Christians there comes the
family, in which new citizens of human society are born.
By the grace of the Holy Spirit received in baptism these
are made children of God, thus perpetuating the People
of God through the centuries. The family is, so to speak,
the domestic Church. In it parents should, by their word
and example, be the first preachers of the faith to their
children . . ." (Dogmatic Constitution on the Church;
p. 11).

So the natural parental role of educator of one's children becomes, for the Christian, a specific work of his lay
priesthood: he is a "preacher of the faith" to his children.

He ought to need no warning that the best testimony he can give to the Truth is not in words, but in deeds, in the quality of life that he creates in his "family church." To aid him in making his community one which is truly a Christian one, a joyful and loving one, the father of the family has need to do what he can to foster a spirit of prayer, celebration, thanksgiving, in short of supernatural love in his community. He will find help in this task by fostering such Christian activities as grace at meals (in some homes this is sung), by family prayers (that are not a rote duty but a time of familial sharing), and the use of sacramentals or the building up of family customs which become part of the texture of the life of the worshiping community that the family is meant to be.

Of recent years in America we have seen many books and pamphlets published about the liturgical life in the home. These have not only fostered but are also a sign of the increasing interest in Christian family life. The Church has a rich treasury of family sacramentals and family customs to help the father of a family and those under his care to grow in grace and be transformed in Christ. Which of these practices or customs will most suit the needs of any specific family is best left up to the individual parents, but the minimum, it would seem, would be a return to the venerable custom of communal night prayers. The father who is fully conscious of the sacred duty that goes with the dignity of his parenthood will, of course, seek for further means to bring Christian truths alive in the minds and hearts of his children. Special days will be remembered in special ways: for example, the baptismal day of each child may be celebrated and his baptismal candle lighted for a few minutes at the principle meal while his father reads again the baptismal promises.

As God's representative in the home, the father is head of what has been called "the first and most important liturgical community." It is he who must guide his family through the liturgical year, explaining to his children the significance of each season and preparing them, each according to his understanding, for the great feasts. It goes without saying that the life of the home must be a liturgical life, a life lived in accord with the rhythms of the liturgical year. Christ's birth should be celebrated as Christ's birth and not as the time when a secular Santa Claus bestows largesse. To tie Christmas to the department store Santa Claus and Easter to bunnies and chicks is not only to secularize these great feasts of the Church, but to endanger the faith of one's children. For when the child's belief in such fairy tales is shattered, it may be discovered that his faith in the reality of Easter and Christmas has been impaired. At the very least, his confidence in his parents may be wounded. This consideration alone should give us pause, but there is the larger consideration of our duty to Christ which cannot be ignored if we wish even to begin to live as Christians.

Practically all the religious practices concerned with the home call for the father's leadership, whether it be the leading of the family prayers, the saying of grace or the blessing of an Advent wreath. The father is the spiritual leader of his sacred community. To refuse to exercise his lay-priesthood, his spiritual leadership, on such occasions either cripples the family's religious life or throws the burden upon the mother—as all too often happens. This can be disastrous since it makes the boys of the family susceptible to the argument they will undoubtedly hear later that "religion is for women."

While we must save details of specific religious customs and sacramentals for the home—leaving these considerations now to the discretion of the father and mother who will find abundant material available on the subject—there is one practice that is so simple that no family could find it difficult to use, so beautiful that it demands our attention and so full of meaning that a discussion of the priestly role of the father would not be complete without it. The custom is that of the parental blessing.

In our home the parental blessing is given by having

the children, in order of age, come to the holy water font after their evening prayers. There each child receives the sign of the cross on his forehead with holy water while the following words are spoken: "I bless you,———, my child, in the name of the Father and of the Son and of the Holy Ghost, Amen." Then follows an aspiration to the child's patron saint.

An alternative, longer blessing, may be used: "May the Almighty God, Father, Son, and Holy Ghost, bless you my child, for time and eternity, and may this blessing remain forever with you, Amen."

Actually, the father may use whatever words he thinks suitable for the occasion, even as the blessing itself need not be restricted to bed-times. A child about to undergo surgery, to attend camp, go hunting, begin school, graduate, be married, could receive the parental blessing. Nor need the practice be discontinued as the child progresses in years. Bishops have been known to kneel for their mother's blessing. That "man for all seasons," St. Thomas More, when Lord Chancellor of England, knelt for his father's blessing each morning.

What a mark of the father's dignity! What an exercise of his lay-priesthood! What man would not be humbled by his recognition of the profound responsibility such a power, the power of blessing his children, lays upon him. What man could bless his children and not himself feel blessed at having children? And what child could kneel for his father's blessing and not recognize that they are tied by a bond stronger than the flesh—that the father is here God's representative? And the father, seeing himself as a channel of grace, is made more aware of his own reliance upon the grace of God, of his own responsibilities before God. The child who goes to bed with the touch of his father's hands upon his head and words of his father's blessing still with him, is a child secure in the knowledge of the love not only of his earthly father but of his Father in Heaven.

Many Catholic fathers, though, seem unwilling to assume their rightful role as leaders in the spiritual life of their families. These prefer to make the Mass an individualistic act of worship rather than a familial one, and as for the sacramentals in the home, they don't want to be "different." They prefer to be indifferent. They like to assume that by having their children in a parochial school they have fulfilled their obligation as far as their spiritual guidance is concerned. They are wrong. The religious training of the school is a training in facts, a training based upon the assumption that at home those facts are placed by the parents into the context of everyday life. No amount of text book knowledge of the Mass will be meaningful if the parents have not awakened a real spirit of sacrifice and thanksgiving in their children. And how do we explain the Mass as a "corporate act of worship" if that most basic corporate unit, the family, does not worship together? How will a child learn any respect for the ordained priest in the pulpit if the lay priest who is his father neglects his duties, rejects the dignity of being "a sharer in the priesthood of Christ the High Priest."

St. Paul speaks of our making up what is lacking in the sufferings of Christ. A startling statement, but it tells us that we must carry Christ to others, must help to apply the merits of His sacrifice to the world. We must do this, lest we be forced to apply to ourselves those words in the last Gospel of the Mass: "He through whom the world was made, was in the world, and the world treated him as a stranger. He came to what was His own, and they who were His own gave Him no welcome." There are homes, too many homes, where Christ has no welcome, where the liturgical year is unknown, the great feasts pass by with only a nod, the family would be embarrassed to pray together and Christ is a stranger in the conversations and plans of the family. These are the homes where the father of the family has either never recognized his lay-priesthood or never chosen to exercise it. These are homes without a spiritual leader.

When our children are in the state of grace, as they

surely are after baptism and before they have reached the age of reason, they are truly holy persons. In them, as in anyone who is in the state of grace, resides the triune God. This indwelling presence of the Holy Trinity is only driven out of the soul by the commission of sin, the rejection of God. Sin is where God is not. When we confront this reality, when we grasp this notion of what living in the state of grace means, that it means sharing in a very real way in the life of God Himself, we cannot but sense the sacredness of our parental vocation. God has not only granted to us the unspeakable privilege of sharing with Him in creation, by allowing us to help in the formation of human persons, but he has given us the sacred trust of raising up these persons as fit temples for His own presence on earth and sharers in His eternal life forever. This is the holy work which we, as parents, are called upon to perform and this is, at root, the reason why our homes are considered "sacred places" by the Church. This, too, is the reason that St. Augustine called the fathers of families: "My fellow bishops . . ."

What a glorious title is ours if we bring Christ into our homes, St. John tells us: "But all those who did welcome Him, He empowered to become the children of God, all those who believe in his name; their birth came, not from human stock, not from nature's will or man's but from God." (John 1:12-13)

Chapter   V

THE FATHER AS TEACHER

"Since parents have given children their life, they are bound by the most serious obligation to educate their offspring and therefore must be recognized as the primary and principal educators. This role in education is so important that only with difficulty can it be supplied where it is lacking. Parents are the ones who must create a family atmosphere animated by love and respect for God and man, in which the well-rounded personal and social education of children is fostered. Hence the family is the first school of the social virtues that every society needs. It is particularly in the Christian family, enriched by the grace and office of the sacrament of matrimony, that children should be taught from their early years to have a knowledge of God according to the faith received in Baptism, to worship Him, and to love their neighbour. Here, too, they find their first experience of a wholesome human society and of the Church. Finally, it is through the family that they are gradually led to a companionship with their fellowmen and with the people of God. Let parents, then, recognize the inestimable importance a truly Christian family has for the life and progress of God's own people."

(*Christian education, No. 3*).

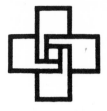

ALL MEN, especially when they are children, need heroes: people whom they honor for outstanding qualities and whose accomplishments give them some guide whereby to judge their own success or failure. For the Christian there is but one Hero, one Person worthy of emulation, the Savior of Mankind, the Lord of History, the Son of God, Jesus Christ. For the Christian all true heroism is rooted in the imitation of Christ and all true heroes are saints, those Christians who most effectively made their lives an imitation of His.

But for the child, his first heroes will be his own parents, particularly the father, he who holds the position of authority in the family. Thus, even a very young child will put on his father's slippers or pick up his pipe and try to sit in the posture of his father. Few parents are unfamiliar with some revealing episode in the play of their children when one child has assumed the role of the father in some given situation and mouthed his exact words! More universal even than that is the commonplace occurrence of the child at table desirous of a fork because "Daddy has a fork," or a "glass like Daddy's."

The father's place as hero in the lives of his children is one that rests upon his positive and clear leadership of the home. If he has shrugged off his decisive role, if he has relegated his authority to the limbo to which he consigns all that he is "too busy" to do, or has allowed his business interests to cut him off from his family, then his children will seek a hero elsewhere. The child does this because he needs authority, he needs a guide; and that authority and that guide must be a person. Children, especially the very young, do not reach rational conclusions and then set their wills upon the accomplishment of ends they deem good. The Church has traditionally maintained that a child does not reach the age of reason and the exercise of free will until his sixth year. Before that time, and even after it for many children, their apprehension of the good and the bad in human life, their ideals and their actions, are patterned upon the very concrete data offered by those around them. They look about for a norm, for somebody to follow and if they do not find that norm in their father, then they will surely find it in one of the many storybook heroes on the TV screen.

Some time ago our newspapers carried the report of a man who had accidentally wounded his infant son while practicing a "fast draw" with a six shooter. The investigation which followed led to the discovery that his front room was full of bullet holes from previous attempts to outdraw the villain of the TV western. Gradually, it came to light that this man was not alone, but that he had his counterparts all across the country, men who were doing their best to imitate the mythic heroes of the TV western. While psychiatric examination in particular cases might reveal other factors, I think that one could safely generalize that these men suffer from a malady peculiar to "post-Christian" man: lacking true heroes to worship, they have chosen to emulate the activities of artificial heroes. If grown men mistake these false heroes for true, how much more readily an unsophisticated child will do the same.

That the father has to compete with pseudo-heroes, whose job is easy because it lasts but a brief few minutes each week while the father's heroism must be consistently observable in his every contact with his family, is a real hazard and has struck a blow at the emulation of the father as hero. Yet, it is a hazard that can and must be met. The solution lies not only in a much more judicious use of the TV, but in reforming our own lives so that they conform more perfectly to that of Christ whose vicar we are in the home. It is not any artificial pose we are called upon to assume—children, lacking guile themselves, are quick to spot deceit in others—but a true union of our own lives with the life of Christ. Pius XII exhorted: "Fathers and mothers, whose natural love is sanctified by the faith of Christ, see that before your child is born you prepare a pure family atmosphere in which it may open its eyes to light and its soul to life, so that the good odour of Christ may linger about every step of its moral development."

"Before your child is born . . ." Some modern psychologists contend that the psychic states of the parents at the time of conception have a tremendous influence upon the personality of the child; some go so far as to claim that the basic personality of the child is formed by the time it is three years old. Without accepting these claims—indeed, rejecting outright those based on a denial of free will and the workings of divine grace—we can yet see the truth underlying them: the first months and years of a child's life exert immeasurable influence over the future development of the human person. "It is your task," Pius XII went on, "from the cradle to begin their education in soul as well as in body; for if you do not educate them they will begin, for good or ill, to educate themselves."

How many children in America are thrown back upon their own resources, are educating themselves because they are not being educated by their parents? A scanning of the morning newspaper is unscientific but sufficient evidence that the education of too many has been self-education and, for that reason, an education in selfishness.

In his great encyclical on the Mystical Body of Christ, Pope Pius XII referred to little children as those "whose innocence is so easily exposed to danger these days and whose little hearts are wax to be moulded." It is in the moulding of the wax of young lives that the fathers of families enjoy one of their highest privileges. Even as they are co-creators with God of this human person, so they are cooperators with God in that high artistry which strives to form Christ in the child. The artist is called *homo faber*, man the maker. What more prodigious making is there than that which collaborates with God in the making of a man! As St. John Chrysostom wrote: "What greater work is there than training the mind and forming the habits of the young!" And this work is first and foremost the work of the father of the family.

In his encyclical on *The Christian Education of Youth*, Pius XI quotes St. Thomas who said: "The father according to the flesh has in a particular way a share in that principle which in a manner universal is found in God. . . . The father is the principle of generation, of education and discipline and of everything that bears upon the perfecting of human life." But this high dignity which is ours as fathers, a dignity and a right which the Church has consistently defended against every attempt at usurpation, is in the words of Pius XI "inseparably joined to the strict obligation." No Christian father should neglect this duty. His fatherhood does not stop short at the mere generation of a child, but continues until that child is prepared morally and intellectually to meet the challenges of life on his own—as an adult.

The infantilism of the hero-worship displayed by the man mentioned earlier in this chapter reflects more upon his father than upon himself. His father apparently never filled the need in his son's life for a hero on the human level, nor pointed out to him that there were more important indications of a man's strength and integrity than how quickly one could pull a six shooter from a holster. A whole generation is growing up that knows only such criteria for the judging of a man, his ability with a gun or his fists, or—not too much differently—with a baseball bat. The "wax" is being moulded by hands other than the father's, the minds and hearts of the young are being formed by advertisers and money-seekers without consciences. The children are looked upon by those who manipulate them through magazines, TV and the movies as a "market," and the moment the market for Roy Roger's equipment is overstocked, Daniel Boone takes over, and when the coon-skin cap market has passed its peak, Maverick's six shooters are put on the merchant's shelves for the hands of children.

"See to it," our Lord warned, "that you do not treat one of these little ones with contempt; I tell you, they have angels of their own in heaven, that behold the face of my heavenly Father continually." (Matt. 18:10) This warning should take root in the hearts of parents, particularly of fathers, for in neglecting their young, casting their children upon outside forces and letting them be moulded willy-nilly by circumstances, they cannot escape the fact that they are treating their children with "contempt."

The home was once a barrier against the outside world. In it, in its quiet and closeted atmosphere, the work of educating the young could go on apace without competition. When the radio and then TV entered the home, all of the outside world flowed, for better and for worse, into the front room. Where the father of a family used to read the Bible in the evening, an announcer now reads a teleprompter and extols the virtues of Nair for removing unsightly hair. Where before a child could be protected in his innocence and made aware gradually and in keeping with his advancement in age of the evil outside his doors, he is today introduced, even before he can read, to the spectacle of head-bashings, torture, strangulation, murder, attempted rape, and seduction. That many of these things have the sop of a "happy ending"—the bad man gets killed, commits suicide or is electrocuted—does not repair the damage done to the young spirit at such a tender age. "And if anyone hurts the conscience of one of these little ones, that believe in me, he had better have been drowned in the depths of the sea, with a mill-stone hung about his neck." (Matt. 18:6)

The reaction of the Christian father must not be merely negative—though no TV would be better than uncontrolled TV—but to be truly effective, it must flow from the father's recognition of his positive responsibilities as teacher. The training of a child requires more than a constant negation of the child's wrongdoing, it demands that the father be a positive influence in the home, put forth positive efforts to educate those who belong to him. Wax is not moulded by merely protecting it from melting, it must be worked upon with a conscious design. So in moulding the young we must ourselves know what we are training them to become. Our primary duty, let us never forget, is to help them become saints. Secondarily, we must see to it that they will be able to take a place among the society of mature men. These two are not opposed; in fact good citizenship among the community of men is a by-product of sanctity.

It goes without saying that the father who recognizes his headship as coming from Christ, who strives to pay special attention to the Christ in those around him, who has brought the life of Christ as it is lived and renewed throughout the liturgical year into the home and who exercises his prerogative to bless his children, has already made progress in the proper education of his children. He is preparing that family atmosphere which Pope Pius XII called for, "in which (the child) may open its eyes to light and its soul to life."

Still, there is more that can be done. The birth of a child marks the start of that child's long training which will prepare him adequately for time and for eternity—and this training is the responsibility of the father of the family. The father should be a teacher although the role of teacher is not a separate occupation for the father. Even as his other roles as breadwinner, priest, creator are not compartmentalized but flow from the one person that he is, so his function as teacher is inextricably woven into the whole pattern of his existence, his way of being. Our role as teachers is not one that requires us to put a desk and blackboard into a certain room and begin to prepare lectures for our children. No, our teaching is one that flows from the very beings we are and takes place, whether we wish it or not, in every contact between ourselves and our children. As fathers we have in our homes growing youngsters whose larger questions may very well be un-asked questions and to them we are unconsciously sup-plying and denying answers every day we live with them. If we are to our pagan neighbors Christianity incarnate, we are to our children much more. If our neighbor judges the Catholic Church by us, then our children get their picture of the entire world from us. Their norm for hu-man relations will be our own relations with them, their mother and others. Telling the children verbally to respect priests will have little effect if we tell them in other ways that we feel superior, intellectually or socially, to the pastor God has given us. On the other hand, to have priest visitors in the home, to kneel for the blessing of a priest before he leaves is to imprint upon our children's minds the image of respect for God's ministers that time will not dim.

So, the example of our own lives will be the greatest teacher. Still, there are other means of education. In the home where Christ is welcome, where religion is a way of life and not another organization we belong to, the children themselves will provide ample opportunity for the father to give them some doctrinal training. A father should not wince at the questions of the young; childish though they may be, they are yet of importance to the child and the father can use them as a further opportunity to forward the spiritual and intellectual growth of his children.

A child's mind is undaunted by mystery. He will ask about the Incarnation, for instance, though not in those words. One of our children, having received the informa-tion that God the Father was spirit, therefore invisible, wanted to know why we could see Jesus. If He was God, why wasn't He spirit? Such questions as these call for ac-curate answers suitable to the mind of the child, and since they come without advance warning and with the child's insistence on an immediate answer, they keep one on his theological toes. Questions flow from the children's attendance at Mass, from the conversations they overhear, from the Bible stories they are read; they are not artificially stimulated. The young mind is an inquiring mind trying to come to grips with the world into which it has been born. The task of the father is to keep that mind inquiring—not to cut off its questions—and yet to help it attain that grip on reality which it seeks.

When it comes to a choice between giving a correct answer that may not be fully understood or "begging the question" by some means, the former alternative is to be preferred. Beware of telling "pious fairy tales"—especially terrifying ones—to illustrate a point. I know of one apostate who traces the crumbling of his faith to the little stories some nun told him to impress upon his mind certain doctrines. Whether she distinguished clearly in her own mind between the doctrine and the story is of no importance, for the child did not. The stories haunted him, he even had nightmares about them. When he grew old enough to see the stories as patently false, as "morality tales" without foundation, his faith suffered a crippling blow.

On no account should we ever use God as a threat, as a "bogey-man" to frighten a child into obedience. Our constant emphasis should be upon God's love for us and our love for Him. A child is naturally loving, seeks love, wants to be constantly assured of the fact that he is loved. He requires all the love that can be given him for the simple reason that he senses his own dependence. The world for him is a world of giants and wonders, a world full of fearful mysteries that he can meet with confidence only if he is confident of being loved himself. To instill in his mind the image of an awful monster called "God," greater even than his own parents, who is going to punish him for every wrongdoing, is to cast love aside and fill his soul with fear. To root the child's relationship with God in fear may do untold damage to the future spiritual life of that child.

In this regard might be mentioned the tremendous responsibility we, as fathers, have in regard to the image our children will have of God, the Church, of all authority. How can a child understand the concept of the loving fatherhood of God if his own father is not loving? How can a child understand that he is free to go to his heavenly Father with his problems and hopes if his earthly father, living in his own home, looks upon him as a nuisance? Too, we should remember that the way in which we exercise our authority at home will determine to a tremendous degree the way in which the child will react to all authority. If we fail to exercise our authority at all, are too indulgent, we shall do our children a grave injustice. Children need authority. When they do not find it at home, they will seek it elsewhere, in older companions, in the entertainment they see, the gang they go with. The very totalitarian organization of the ever-expanding number of youth gangs roaming the streets of our major cities today is a commentary upon the lack of authority in the homes of the gang members. On the other hand, if we are arbitrary, unjust, dictatorial, if we discipline for our own selfish ends, the child will soon rebel. And his rebellion may not stop with a mere rebellion against his father's authority, but may express itself in a rebellion against all authority. At the least, the man who exercises his authority for his own selfish ends—every instruction a negative command or a prohibition—will soon find his children are strangers to him. They will await his departure from the house that they may live more exuberantly; they will dread his homecoming and they will—if older—eagerly await the time when they can leave home. If he punishes them unjustly, in anger or out of proportion to their offense, he will find their acquiescence to him is rooted in fear and their respect for him is a respect merely for his brute strength. His authority, his teachings, being selfish at root, will be obeyed only when he is present to enforce them.

The whole matter of wrongdoing and its punishment should be modeled after God's own treatment of His children. Should our children do wrong, we can attempt to find out if their wrongdoing was deliberate, accidental, caused by some desire to do good, whether the child is sorry, willing to "make up" in the case of a child's squabble, etc. Then, given the situation that the child has done something he knows to be wrong, we can punish according to the gravity of the situation. Sometimes the children can be allowed to exercise their own freedom in choosing which privilege they wish to forego—dessert, story, movie, allowance, etc.,—as penance. But once the proper balance has been restored, the child should be made aware that he is once again on a good footing with all concerned. He should not be harassed about the event, nor should the other children be allowed to taunt him about it. It is the wise, the patient father who can remind himself in time that young children do not possess full powers of reason, are not capable of the full exercise of free will. On the other hand, he must remember that Original Sin's consequences are always cropping up and that he must try to channel and train the will and the conscience of his children.

But our approach should here be more positive than negative. Praise for good motives and correct behavior is as necessary to our children as the correction of their wrongs. We should be as alert to virtue in them as to faults, as quick to praise as to blame. Children crave attention and they desire our approval. If we ignore them when they are good on the grounds that that is expected and give them attention only when they do wrong, they will sacrifice approval for that attention.

That to his younger children he is infallible should not make the father feel that he must live up to this impossible image. Our education of our children is an education for reality and it is both unwise and unrealistic for the father to attempt to live up to the impossible image of the perfect and all-knowing human being. Even if the relationship of father and child somehow escaped being uneasy or unhuman, even if the father somehow were able to maintain the illusion for a time, the day of recognition of his father's clay feet could have a shattering effect upon the young child. On the other hand, the wise father, while remembering that to his children he is a hero, will, like the knights of old and those great heroes the saints, remember to refer all things to God. A mistake, a wrong turn on some outing, a forgotten promise to bring home some ice cream, can be an occasion when the father can remind his children of his own humanity—of the fact that God alone does not make mistakes and is not forgetful.

The relationship of fathers and children should be, therefore, a relationship in love even as our relationship with God should be a relationship in love. God's command to children to honor their parents is not without its requirements upon parents; it is a command to them to live and to exercise their authority in such a way that they are worthy of honor and of love. They must be able to say with Christ, "my yoke is easy, and my burden is light." (Matt. 11:30)

Of many parents it may be said that their children find their yoke a difficult yoke and their burden a heavy burden—probably because the parents themselves look upon their children as a yoke and a burden neither sweet nor light. Such parents normally see everything their children request or desire to do as a threat to their "time" or "energy." They quickly lapse into the habit of saying "no" to all that a child might ask. They respond negatively without considering what the request is, what it may mean to the child, or whether it may be just as easy to say "yes." Thus, a child might ask to go to bed with one stocking on—because Deedle Deedle Dumpling in the Mother Goose book did—and the parent says "no." There is no valid reason behind the denial although, in the child's mind, there was a real reason behind the request. The stocking will not be damaged or lost by being worn to bed, the child will be happy with it on, there will be no great effort about finding it in the morning should it have slipped off. The prompt "no" means the child has lost another opportunity to assert his own proper will, to do something that he wanted to do.

One of the most important works of the parents is the training of the child in the proper use of its free will, and here is a case where the child might have been allowed that freedom of choice. While it is sometimes easier to say "no" without considering the request on its merits, it might be wiser and more worthwhile to say "yes" once in a while and, by this means, help the child toward independence of action.

This is not a call for a child-centered home in the sense that the children get everything they want—as is too often the case in America—but rather a suggestion that parents not overlook the self-training of their children in their own making of decisions and the acceptance of the consequences. Thus, while in our family it is up to the parents to decide whether the children will have ice cream, the children get the opportunity to choose their flavor. If a dispute arises, Amy having chosen chocolate and Michael strawberry but each wanting vanilla like Mommy got, they are made to abide by their choices. This approach can be applied to innumerable situations, but always the lesson is the same: when freedom of choice is allowed, the consequences must be accepted.

As children grow older, the problem becomes more complex, is less susceptible of easy answers. What does a parent do when confronted by a seventeen year old full of all the explosive force of adolescence, capable of going right or left, up or down? What can the father confronted by such a son do? Well, the question is wrongly phrased. The fact of the matter is that if he has not already done it, he is not going to be able to do anything now except pray earnestly. If, on the other hand, he has always maintained an open relationship with his child, if "business" and other selfishness have not clogged the channels of communication, if the son and the father have always loved and respected one another as persons, worthy of one another's love and respect, then the seventeen year old will have little trouble in approaching his father and discussing his problems and plans. Seventeen is an age of plans; adolescence is not just an age of juvenile delinquency. Adolescence is also the age of highest idealism, when young men feel they can climb the highest mountain, write the greatest book, remould the botched up world that has been handed them. If we admit that the temptations and the forces at work in adolescence are powerful things, we must also admit that the idealism of adolescence is a beautiful thing.

But between the small child and the older adolescent is another and even more trying period. The first realization that some of his ideals, perhaps his home life itself, are not common to all, will cause him to question—he does not want to be different. Each father must seek how best to meet this crisis for his own particular child. At certain ages the desire to be one of the crowd is an intense, psychological necessity. There are many areas where this imitativeness may be allowed: to have the same kind of lunch pail, to get a certain haircut. The granting of such reasonable requests can help keep the child from feeling that the area of negation or the degree of difference is overwhelming. The wise father will strive not merely to negate this or that harmful public practice, but to replace it by a Christian and positive one. Much depends upon the actual circumstances of the case, and the temperament of the child, but the father might have recourse to the fact that Christians are supposed to be different. In fact, the crying shame of this world today is that too many Christians are indistinguishable from their pagan neighbors.

The problem of sexual instruction is one that troubles many parents. Those who think that the matter can be solved by holding a father-son talk on some specified day —"Now you can be told, my boy"—or that the matter will be covered by the teacher of religion, are naive. Sex instruction is not a matter of facts so much as it is an attitude towards one's own person and towards all created things. There was no "sex problem" in this regard in the

Middle Ages for the very simple reason that the Catholic Church has a healthy attitude towards the human body. It took Puritanism to change the attitudes, even of many Catholics, towards the body, towards created things. If we have brought our children up cognizant of the goodness of all created things, of the great dignity conferred upon the human body when "the Word became Flesh," our task will not be so difficult. Too, if they have had each of their questions answered as it was asked, they will reach young adulthood with most of the fundamental facts. Again, the facts should be accurate, even though they must be simplified for the child. The child should neither be given a sense of shame about his genitals, nor should he be given any more information than needed to satisfy his curiosity of the moment.

The approach must always center upon the sacredness of the body, of the high purpose of sex, of the glorious wonder that men and women can "help God" in creation. The parent has no need of embarrassment or of fear. When the occasions arise, when the child is curious about this or that aspect of sex, the parent has only to use his common sense in transmitting to the child the truth concerning the marvelous and beautiful way in which God has made us. The important thing is that the parent himself know and fully realize the sacredness and beauty of human sexuality. If he does, then he will have little trouble bringing to his children the facts of human reproduction in a manner that will foster in them a reverence towards their own bodies and a respect for the sacrament of matrimony.

We found that allowing the children to watch their cat have kittens inspired them with wonder. They know that little kittens are kept inside their mother's "tummy" until they get big enough to live outside. There is no more normal and healthy way for children to learn the secrets of nature. Also, having seen their mother breastfeed the latest arrival, they know what breasts are for—a knowledge apparently esoteric and all but forgotten in our society.

The child who has always received correct and adequate answers to his questions generally will not hesitate to bring further questions when they arise. His knowledge of the "facts of life" will grow with his own growth, keeping pace with his own curiosity and ability to receive the truth. For such a child adolescence and its concommitant turmoil will not be as difficult as for that child who has been taught that his body is "nasty" and who has discovered from some older lad that his parents did "nasty" things to bring him into the world. For the former child all the new stirrings in his body and his mind will find their proper place in his world, in his understanding of God's goodness; temptations will be seen as temptations; purity will have a solid grounding in all his previous training and in Truth. For the latter child, adolescence will become a vile pit—from which he may not escape.

Our training of our children in doctrine and morality, a training that goes on all the time, is not merely an education for eternity. The natural law is natural; that is, it is suited to the needs of man on the natural plane. The divine law does not take away from the natural law, but fulfills it. By training our children for eternal life with God, we are training them in virtues which prepare them to cope adequately with the conditions of life on earth. Only the knowledge of Christ can give men hope in the face of the perils of nuclear warfare. Only the teachings of the Catholic Church and the use of the sacraments entrusted to it can bring order and peace to this earth. Not only is there no conflict between being a good Christian and being a good citizen but St. Augustine could say, "Let those who declare the teaching of Christ to be opposed to the welfare of the state, furnish us with an army of soldiers such as Christ says soldiers ought to be; let them give us subjects, husbands, wives, parents, children, masters, servants, kings, judges, taxpayers, and taxgatherers who live up to the teachings of Christ; and then let them dare assert that Christian doctrine is harmful to the state. Rather let them not hesitate one moment to acclaim that doctrine, rightly observed, the greatest safeguard of the state." If we bring up our children formed to the image of Christ, we will have brought them up ready not only for the battles of this age in which we live, but we will have given to the world some good citizens, people who are a credit to humanity.

Children enter history through the family into which they are born and Americans are losing, if they have not already lost, their sense of family. I know nothing of either of my grandparents, for instance, save one hazy recollection of my mother's mother visiting our home when I was a child. She never visited us again and she died a few years later. I think that in not knowing anything about my grandparents, I am typical of most of my generation. We have no real sense of family lineage, no blood lines, no historical feeling. Personally, I miss this knowledge; I feel it as a lack within me and I am nostalgic for what I feel is my rightful heritage. I am hoping to provide my children with that knowledge of which I (and this is not meant to imply blame upon anyone) was deprived. Through human relationships, mementoes, photos and stories, we hope to awaken in our children an awareness of the family as something more than the people with whom they live. Perhaps we can help them to recognize it for what it is: a living entity which extends back through time and space and forward into the future. Should they gain this sense of family, perhaps they will come to an appreciation of their role as the bearers of a culture and of a tradition, a Christian culture and a Christian tradition. In order for them to feel at home in the world, it seems essential that they have a home in the world. In order for them to recognize their familial ties with all men, it seems necessary for them to have familial ties with some men. I think it is not much less important for them to become familiar with their grandparents, if only from secondary sources, as they are with their parents and will be with their children and their children's children. The man of wisdom is the man with the sense of history. When the man of wisdom not only looks to the past and knows from whence he came, but looks to the future and knows where he is going, he is making that first step towards that knowledge which leads to sanctity.

Our teaching at home is not only a teaching of facts, however. It is the handing on to a child of a whole view, a Christian view, of the universe. This is not so difficult a task as it may at first seem; the wonder of a child at creation is in itself a "Christian" thing. It is a real, profound wonder at the world of concrete beings. The child, in this sense, is a metaphysician and his wonder is kept ever fresh by each new discovery he makes concerning himself or his world. In paying attention to creation, in joying in created things, the child is like St. Francis offering a prayer to God. It is tragic that the sense of wonder, the sense of mystery before God's handiwork is so soon snuffed out in our rushing world, so often immersed under the tide of artificial distractions, amusements, business. The wonder of a child at existence should not be crushed out, either, by any too doctrinaire approach to the realities of faith, morals, the world of human relationships. Especially not by the negative formula approach. Christianity is not a set of prohibitions, it is not a list of negative statements; it is an explosive affirmation of existence, of the goodness of created things, of the glorious destiny that awaits men who have learned to love their fellow men for the love of God.

The task is not easy. The burden is not light. The obligation is grave. The responsibility is as great as that any man can hold: the responsibility for the eternal welfare of a soul. But God has promised all of those joined together in holy matrimony all of the graces necessary for them to fulfill their vocations. The rearing of our children is one of the main tasks of our vocation so God's graces are with us in this holy work. Children are themselves a vehicle of grace for parents. Indeed, children are the models for parents. To look at a young child is to see what purity of heart it is we are asked by Christ to strive for. "Believe me, unless you become like little children again, you shall not enter the kingdom of Heaven. He is greatest in the kingdom of Heaven who will abase himself like this little child." (Matt. 38:3-4) The almost tangible holiness of little children is a holiness that we should do all in our power to protect and nurture as our children grow up, a holiness we can look to as a reminder of what God wants of us. The obedience we ask and expect of our children is the obedience that God asks and expects of us. Their innocence, their directness and honesty, God wants of us. Their dependence upon us for all their needs is but a tiny image of our dependence upon God the Father of all. If we are, in fact, exemplars of the world and of God to our children, they should be for us exemplars of what we are to become if we wish to enter the kingdom of heaven. The teacher who has not the humility to learn from his pupils is not a teacher at all.

Chapter VI

THE FATHER AS BREADWINNER

"It has always been the duty of Christian married partners but today it is the greatest part of their apostolate to manifest and prove by their own way of life the indissolubility and sacredness of the marriage bond, strenuously to affirm the right and duty of parents and guardians to educate children in a Christian manner, and to defend the dignity and lawful autonomy of the family. They and the rest of the faithful, therefore, should co-operate with men of good will to ensure the preservation of these rights in civil legislation and to make sure that governments give due attention to the needs of the family regarding housing, the education of children, working conditions, social security, and taxes; and that in policy decisions affecting migrants their right to live together as a family should be safeguarded."

(*Apostolate of the Laity, No. 11*).

"Give Us this day our daily bread . . ." we pray to our Father in heaven and even as we look to Him, so our family looks to us. The father of the family is normally a "breadwinner." One of his root responsibilities is to provide for his family those basic necessities of life symbolized by bread, "the staff of life." The family owes to the labors of the father all those things without which civilized existence would be impossible: food, clothing, shelter. In less complex times the almost complete reliance of the family upon the labors of the father was more visible; more often than not he nurtured that bread from the very soil he tilled, living out literally the figurative injunction: "Thou shalt earn thy bread by the sweat of thy brow." (Gen. 3:19) And if he labored arduously with rude tools, if for long hours in the hot sun he sweated over the soil, he was rewarded with the sweet pleasure of contemplating a land made fruitful by his own calloused hands, he could dip those hands into the freshly ground wheat before his wife kneaded it into loaves which would be broken at their meal. Both he and his family could see the direct relationship between his labor and their daily life: "Give us this day our daily bread . . ."

Today, the concept of the father as breadwinner has been dislocated. As often as not, the mother and wife contributes as much as the father to the support of the family. But even in those families where the father continues to assume full responsibility as provider, his task has undergone a change. Instead of winning his bread from a soil enriched by his sweat, the average father sweats elsewhere: in an office, behind the wheel of a bus, in front of a lathe or a blast furnace. And he works to earn the money that will purchase the "bread"—the material necessities to sustain his family. In short, he has ceased to be a "breadwinner" in the literal sense of the term and has become a "wage-earner." Between the labors of the father and the food on the table stands the "wage" which he has earned, the money he supplies. And it is here that danger confronts the contemporary family.

That the father sweats in a place foreign, usually, to the gaze of his wife or children, means that his responsibility in supplying the family necessities becomes less visible to their eyes. The family can lose sight of the truly vital link between his labors and the food on the table, for he neither grew nor harvested it and oftentimes he has not even bought it but merely supplied the money with which his wife paid the cashier in the supermarket. Thus, if only subconsciously, but often quite openly, the father is looked upon by his family as that person who pays the bills. This can be serious to a greater or lesser degree; it is most serious when the father himself looks upon his role as solely that of paying the bills.

"I don't know what she wants of me," the man cried out toward the end of his tale of marital strife, "I've given her and the kids everything. I'm breaking my back to do it—just meeting the payments is killing me off, but I don't complain. The doctor tells me to slow down, but how can I slow down? Each month there are all those bills to pay," he looked up, "and they get paid. She and the kids must think I've got a magic wand—but they're killing off the magician."

Another man, whose wife after fourteen years of marriage was suing him for divorce, said, "We had nothing when we were married. Now she's got her own car, the best of everything. If she wanted anything for herself or the kids, all she had to do was write a check. She's never had one bounce."

The first of these men had allowed his family to thrust

him into the role of bill-payer and he did not know how to get out; the second had failed even to glimpse that his paternity involved any more responsibility, any involvement more profound than that of a supplier of material wants. It does not take much insight to see that if the responsibility of the father was only to provide for the material welfare of his family, then the father of a family could easily be replaced by a bank account or a trust fund. But Christ has warned us that it is not by bread alone that man does live.

Surely it is the first duty of a father to supply the material needs of his family. But this responsibility must be viewed in its proper perspective. The material needs of a family are really few. In America most people would not find the task of meeting those needs beyond their powers. Yet the basic worry of American family men seems to be a concern over material things and financial problems are a major cause of marital strife. Too often, such financial problems are due to a confusion between true needs and the false needs aroused by advertisers.

"If any one of yourselves is asked by his son for bread," our Lord asked those men who first heard the Sermon on the Mount, "will he give him a stone?" (Matt. 7:9) What man would do such a thing? Where is the man who hands his sons stones instead of bread? Is he not, perhaps, that one quoted above who gave his family the stones of manufactured goods, bank accounts, blank checks for material purposes? Isn't he the man who is "too busy" with his work to eat even the principal meal of the day with his family? Isn't the man who is so engrossed in earning money outside of the home that he doesn't know what is going on within its walls another who is bringing home stones? That father who thrusts the religious training of his children entirely upon their mother and the nuns has handed his sons the stone which may break their spiritual spines as they grow up thinking of religion as something feminine. That father who is too embarrassed to say grace at meal times has handed his sons a stone—the stone of a sin the moral theologians call "fear of human respect."

But all of us are guilty of giving our children stones instead of bread. How many times have we come home burdened with the day's fatigues and worries and given to our children nothing but the stone of our cold presence, refusing to open ourselves to them, to the healing laughter of their innocence? No, if we examine our consciences, few of us could claim never to have committed this crime. But how many no longer see the difference between stones and bread at all. These are the fathers who think of their fatherhood as a material debt rather than a spiritual one, who believe that as long as the bills are paid, they are meeting their responsibility as breadwinners. Today's newspaper reports of juvenile crimes, adolescent suicides, brutal family atrocities all testify that many men are handing their children not the bread which only a true father can give, but the stones of that anonymous man who pays the bills, the man who could be replaced by a trust fund.

To meet real needs, to feed the hungry, clothe the naked, shelter the homeless: yes, what is our obligation to others in charity is a serious obligation in justice to our family. We are morally bound to provide for them. That bond gives us our right to the heroic title of "breadwinner." But to exert our powers, to exhaust ourselves in the accumulation of money, to strive after all the unneeded luxuries and self-indulgent trivia held out by our advertising industry and to neglect the spiritual welfare of those to whom we have irrevocably bound ourselves, this is to follow the Tempter.

When the Tempter approached our Lord, he said, "If thou art the Son of God, bid these stones be turned into loaves of bread." (Matt. 4:3) This was a double barreled temptation, a temptation to pride and to greed. Satan was asking our Lord to assert His divine power in a vain display, but he also was asking our Lord, Who had been fasting for forty days, to forego His reliance upon the Father and to provide food for Himself. It is this very temptation to ostentation and to a lack of trust in our Heavenly Father that causes many heads of families to devote their energies to money-making. Such breadwinners have allowed themselves to be seduced by the same Tempter whom our Lord thrust aside with the words: "It is written, Man cannot live by bread only; there is life for him in all the words which proceed from the mouth of God." (Matt. 4:4)

The Son of God did not hesitate to multiply loaves and fishes in abundance when a hungry multitude needed nourishment; He was quite capable of turning the very stones to bread, but He left for us a divine example of trust in our heavenly Father and the rejection of proud display. It is an example little heeded in contemporary society where men avid for the amassing and display of wealth allow their work as breadwinners to cut them off either from God or from their families, and, sadly, if a man allows his job to do one of these, it will eventually do the other. Such men bring home not bread, but stones.

We read about these unfortunate men in our newspapers every day. Sometimes we see them photographed in criminal courtrooms, tear-streaked faces turned toward the young stranger at their side, asking: "What did I do wrong?" Often they beg the judge and the world to believe that "I've given him everything." But is not that admission really an answer to their question? In giving their children everything weren't they doing wrong? Everything —if it only means everything of a material nature—is not enough. In fact, everything is too little as long as it does not include a relationship in charity. To give things is not to give love. The things we give to others can only serve as outward signs, symbolic expressions, and often tragically fragile ones, of the ineffable inner commitment to the good of the other which we call love. To give love is to give of ourselves. To love is to exist for the other and the greatest love is to surrender our lives for the good of the loved one.

"Dry throat and parching tongue for babe at breast;

children asking for bread, and never a crust to share with them!" the prophet Jeremias lamented. We can accept his description for those unfortunate enough to have a father who "gave them everything" but forgot the "one thing necessary." The starvation of the body the prophet depicted is but a pale image of that starvation of spirit we read about in every case of juvenile delinquency—our newspapers ache with reports of a world starving for love.

We are men and we live in history. The world we inhabit today is a world enraptured by the material. We are the target of a daily attack on our wills. An hour does not pass without bringing, in some form or another, the blatant or subtle suggestion that this or that product will make us "happy," "successful," or "secure," with the underlying suggestion, of course, that without it we are unhappy, unsuccessful and insecure. Ten billion dollars a year are spent in the endeavor to convince us that our peace will come with the latest products of our assembly lines.

And money, battening on our technological civilization has grown from a mere medium of exchange, a token we use to obtain things we need, to a monstrous thing sought after for its own sake. It has ceased being a means and has become an end. Previously, in his non-money society, man working his soil was limited by the extent of his own energies—one man can do only so much work—and by the horizon of his own needs. Any excess of his fields which could not be bartered off for other necessities would spoil. The very cycle of nature held greed in check. Sheep can be sheared, a crop can be harvested only when nature has readied them for the hand of man. Even if he could afford the time away from his work, a man would be insane to build a home twice as large as he needed; and to burden himself with more horses than he had a use for would have been sheer stupidity. The advent of money and a moneyed economy changed this, removed this natural barrier to man's acquisitiveness. Money, having no contact with nature, being in fact an unnatural thing, could be gathered without cease; it did not spoil, it did not wait upon the seasons, it could be gained, counted, banked, exchanged and otherwise manipulated at all hours of the day or night. Gathering interest, it could even multiply itself!

There is little likelihood—barring the crime of a nuclear war—that our technological civilization will abolish itself, nor do sensible men ask us to turn back the pages of history and deny the many advantages which we enjoy but which our ancestors never fancied. Idyllic daydreams of a past "simple life" often exclude the harsher aspects of the age. Still, that we enjoy advantages which our fathers did not know is no reason to deny that we face challenges and problems that they did not face. Oftentimes these are made the more difficult because they do not present themselves as problems and challenges but only as facts of our daily existence.

One such fact is the terrible tendency of the bread-winner who has become a wage-earner to look upon himself as the materialistic Marx looked upon him—a mere producer or consumer of goods. Another tendency is the thoughtlessness which attributes to money a power which it does not have: the power to fill the abyss created in the human soul when love is absent.

If we give our children only the material goods of this world, we shall starve them to death and, before God, we shall answer for our crime. St. Matthew tells us that our Lord, taking onto his lap a little child said: "He who gives welcome to such a child as this in my name gives welcome to me. And if anyone hurts the conscience of one of these little ones, that believe in me, he had better have been drowned in the depths of the sea, with a mill-stone hung about his neck." (Matt. 18:5-6) It might be time for Christian fathers to examine their consciences, ponder the attitudes which they have adopted from the society in which they live and see if they really want to pass such ideals on to their children.

The Christian father should remember that, although he is a man involved in human history, a man caught up in time, human history was fractured two thousand years ago by the Son of God, who entered time in order to redeem it. Our human history is now Sacred History, for Christ is involved in it. In his marriage, the Christian father knows he mirrors the relationship of Christ with His Church—and even as the Church through baptism brings new souls into the Mystical Body, so too does the Christian father cooperate with God in the creation of new members for that Mystical Body. "It is for God that children are born to men."

We have spoken elsewhere of the educative and priestly aspects of the father's vocation. It should be unnecessary to point out that all of these aspects of fatherhood overlap, that the father is one man and not many and that our arbitrary division of his single role as head of the family is made solely in order better to penetrate the mystery of such headship. It naturally follows that much of what was said concerning the power of the father's own example and the real penetration of the life of the Church into the home will help us here in meeting the call of our children for bread, in fulfilling our duties as breadwinners.

But one thing should be underscored. The best defense against the devil is an offense. If he would use all the weapons of modern technology to stamp upon us the image of twentieth century materialistic man, then we must strive to attain in our own lives that spirit of Christian poverty which Christ counseled us to. We must seek true and pure poverty of spirit. We must remember at all times that the bread that we have on our tables is there by the grace of God. Upon all the goods with which God might reward our labors we must seek his blessing. No family meal should be consumed that has not first been the subject of prayerful thanks to the One who gave it to us—a prayer led by the head of the family, the father, the *alter-Christus* who won for the family by his toils in the world this earthly bread even as Christ won for all men by His suffering that Bread of Everlasting Life which is Himself. "Bless us, O, Lord, and these thy gifts, which of thy bounty we are about to receive, through Christ our Lord . . ." "And may thou provide for the needs of others."

The family table is an image of the communion table. Even as at table a family shares the same life-giving substance so at the communion table all the members of the Mystical Body partake of Him who called Himself "the life." Even as the food and drink the father of the family provides helps his family to health and strength, so our Father in heaven has given us His Son, who said, "my flesh is real food, my blood is real drink" (John 6:56) "The man who eats of my flesh and drinks my blood enjoys eternal life." (John 6:55)

True Christian poverty does not mean destitution. Some of the poorest of men materially have not the spirit of poverty. Neither does true Christian poverty mean that a man must look upon the things of this world as evil— which would be the sin of Manicheanism and an implicit denial of the fulness of the Incarnation. Rather, the Christian father remains detached from the fruits of his labors. He remembers that these things are not important in themselves and that man needs no-thing to be happy, that happiness is found in doing the will of God.

The freedom that comes from such detachment is but a dim reflection of the freedom which Christ himself displays in the Gospels. He could sit at the tables of rich men, He could defend the use of the costliest oils in the anointing of His feet, He could be accused of associating with tax gatherers and wine-bibbers, but He could also say of Himself, "Foxes have holes, and the birds of the air their resting places; the Son of Man has nowhere to lay his head." (Matt. 8:20)

Not all Christians are called upon to renounce the ownership of property, but all are called upon to keep their hearts and wills free from attachment to mere possessions. "I say to you, then, do not fret over your life, how to support it with food and drink; over your body, how to keep it clothed." (Matt. 6:25) "Believe me, a rich man will not enter God's kingdom easily." (Matt. 19:23) "My children, how hard it is for those who trust in riches to enter God's kingdom!" (Mark 10:24) Again and again in the gospels we find Christ returning to the theme: in order for a man to enter the kingdom of heaven he must remember that: "No servant can be in the employment of two masters at once; either he will hate the one and love the other, or he will devote himself to one and despise the other. You must serve God or money; you cannot serve both." (Luke 16:13)

Recently, during one of the great California forest fires, a young executive left his office to race to his foothill home and rescue what he might. Along the highway, where the road turned off into the hills, he met his wife. She informed him that the fire was a few hundred yards from their barn, but their home was sure to be destroyed. Upon arrival, he told her to let out the dog and the cats from the house while he ran to free the horses from their stables. When his wife returned to his side, she asked, "What shall we save now?" And the man said, "Nothing."

Back on the highway, the man explained that on the drive to the home he had been anxiously cataloguing in his mind all of the possessions which he must rescue from the blaze. Before reaching his wife, he had decided that they had a duty to the living creatures, the horses, dog and cats, but that all of the rest was unimportant. "We don't need things to be happy," he told his wife. "We must not lose our freedom to things." So they drove back to the city, took a room in a hotel and waited for the fire to be brought under control. When they returned to their homesite, they found that the wind had averted the fire but a few yards from their home. Their house and all of their possessions were intact. "Perhaps if I had tried to save those things," the man said later, "I would have lost them all—God's way of showing me their unimportance."

One wishes more people could see the truth this man saw, could recognize that while material things are good, they are gifts of God and the gifts are not to be placed above the Giver. They are tokens of His love, but who would prefer the token to the lover? What bride, showing her wedding ring, would not consider insane the question of which she loved the most, her ring or her husband? All that we have, our very existence itself, we have as the free gift of God. All that is given, is given to bring us closer to Him. And yet, even in Christ's day people missed the fundamental fact, preferred the gift to the Giver. St. John tells us how our Lord was sought out by the multitude he had the day before fed with the five barley loaves and two fishes. And when the crowds found Jesus, He said to them: "Believe me, if you are looking for me now, it is not because of the miracles you have seen; it is because you were fed with the loaves, and had your fill." (John 6:26)

The crowd had accepted the gift and missed its meaning, had failed to understand the spiritual message behind the miraculous act, had not seen this prodigious event as an example of God's goodness, His gift-giving, His "bounty." Instead they had accepted the bread as mere physical nourishment and He who had filled their stomachs they wanted to make their king. Human nature has undergone no change. We live in the midst of crowds who do not know enough to thank God for the food which He has given them, and who allow the material goods of this life to stand between them and God, rather than to be a constant reminder of His solicitude. And the words which Christ directed to the crowd are an attempt to correct this attitude. "You should not work to earn food which perishes in the using. Work to earn food which affords continually, eternal life, such food as the Son of Man will give you: God, the Father, has authorized Him." (John 6:27)

This entire sixth chapter of St. John's Gospel should be read, it is too lengthy to quote in full here. It reminds those of us who are busy about the work of earning the daily bread for our tables that this natural bread, like the bread that Moses gave, the manna in the desert, is not the "real bread from heaven." The men who ate the manna in the desert, our Lord said, "died none the less; the bread which comes down from heaven is such that he who eats of it never dies. I myself am the living bread that has come down from heaven. If anyone eats of this bread, he shall live for ever." (John 6:49-52)

As the breadwinners of families, we should meditate often upon these words and this chapter of the Gospel. The bread we win, that natural bread that graces our tables, important as it is to the bodily health of ourselves and our families, should be for us a symbol, even as the "manna" was, of "the real bread from heaven . . . given only by the Father." (John 6:32) And that Bread is Christ the Lord. "God's gift of bread comes down from heaven and gives life to the whole world." (John 6:33)

Chapter VII

THE FATHER AS SAINT

Christian spouses in virtue of the sacrament of Matrimony, whereby they signify and partake of the mystery of that unity and fruitful love which exists between Christ and His Church, help each other to attain to holiness in their married life and in the rearing and education of their children. By reason of their state and rank in life they have their own special gift among the people of God."

(Dogmatic constitution on the Church, No. 11).

"Married couples and Christian parents should follow their own proper path (to holiness) by faithful love. They should sustain one another in grace throughout the entire length of their lives. They should imbue their offspring, lovingly welcomed as God's gift, with Christian doctrine and the evangelical virtues. In this manner, they offer all men the example of unwearying and generous love; in this way they build up the brotherhood of charity; in so doing, they stand as the witness and co-operators in the fruitfulness of Holy Mother Church; by such lives, they are a sign and a participation in that very love, with which Christ loved His Bride and for which He delivered Himself up for her."

(Dogmatic constitution on the Church, No. 41).

"The Great Adventurers of the modern world." With these words Charles Péguy honored the heads of families. Péguy was killed in the first of the modern world's global wars, but if he were alive today he would probably feel the need to underscore his statement. What soldier of fortune faces a greater challenge than that confronted by the father navigating the ship of his family through the currents of modern life? Erupting from the depths of life's sea, raging storms—seen only as warnings on the barometer in Péguy's day—have now begun to crash fully against the seams of the family ark, tearing at its white sails of holiness, pounding against its bulwarks which are the unity and indissolubility of marriage. If at any given time the head of the family underestimates the danger or fails to respond adequately to the challenge, his ship may flounder.

"The great adventurers of the modern world," indeed. And called to an adventure of no little importance: the pitting of ourselves against all of the enemies of paternity; the warding off of all the daily advances of a multi-billion dollar advertising industry devoted to making us and our children avaricious, lustful, proud; all of this, yes, but more. Ours is not only a defensive action, we must at the same time take the offensive. We fight against storms, but for the sake of arriving at our destination. The enemy without must be held off, while each day sees new attacks on the enemy within. If we, as laymen, have the burden of Christianizing our secular society, if we, as the heads of families, have the obligation of making our homes holy places, we must become Christ-like, we must be saints.

For those who think of sanctity in terms of the canon-
ized, or as the special province of those who have been
called to the religious life, this blunt statement may come
as a surprise. Yet the words of Christ to us are even more
forceful: "But you are to be perfect, as your heavenly
Father is perfect." (Matt. 5:48) These words were not
uttered to any individual selected from among the apostles, nor even to the apostles alone, but to a "great multitude," (Matt. 4:25) a multitude so great that "Jesus, when
he saw how great was their number, went up on to the
mountainside" (Matt. 5:1) in order to speak to them.
There can be no denying that we are included in the multitude, that the Lord's words are for all men throughout all
time. Each of us is called to a life of perfection that has
no limits.

Some men dismiss the call as unrealistic, asking, "How
can I hope to achieve perfection when I'm so caught up
in daily cares, when the children demand so much time,
when the job leaves me completely fatigued?" Others try
to live the life of a monk with one part of their being and
the life of a layman committed to temporal chores with
the other. Such an endeavor, not too uncommon, can lead
a man to look upon those with whom he lives and works
as so many obstacles in his path to God, as hindrances to
his contemplation and as distractions from his prayers.
Such men often begin to evidence a real impatience with
others that expresses itself in self-righteous indignation.
In most cases they soon give up the struggle and join that
group of men who have decided beforehand that sanctity
is impossible under the circumstances of their lives. Some
few persist, though, determined to succeed in spite of
family or friends; steeling their hearts, they seal themselves off in their own rooms for hours at a time for prayer
and contemplation and think they are succeeding in their
spiritual life when they have gotten their family to keep
quiet during such times.

What all these fail to realize is that the call to sanctity
is one conditioned to their state of life: as fathers of fami-

lies it is in and through our paternity that we are to achieve our fullest perfection. Not in spite of marriage and our family life will we grow in grace, but because of them. Our parental work, when performed in Christ, is our holy work, as holy a work as that of any religious who labors to educate the young, nurse the ill, house the homeless or otherwise care for God's children. There is particular relevance for us, as fathers, in that incident in our Lord's life reported by St. Mark: "And he took a little child, and gave it a place in the midst of them; and he took it in his arms, and said to them: Whoever welcomes such a child as this in my name, welcomes me; and whoever welcomes me, welcomes, not me, but him that sent me." (Mark 9:35-36)

To marry is to undertake, as Father Theodore Mackin, S. J., Chairman of the Theology Department of the University of Santa Clara, put it, "a career of finding divine knowledge and love where it is at work in, and shaped by, the personality of one's spouse; and of bringing one another to the beatific vision through a career of the faint and preliminary experiences of this vision available in the happiest moments of marriage." It is in and through the experiences of marriage, then, and in the labors of rearing a family, of "welcoming" God Himself in the children that He has given us, that we are to be made holy. We were called the married state, not to a life of contemplation. We are laymen and our care for our families is a care that binds us to the temporal. We are not priests who bring God into the world, we are lay-priests who bring the world to God. Our daily work, our bread-winning, our house-painting, bill-paying, bed-time reading, can be made holy if we do these things as an offering of love to the Lord. To make of our daily lives an offering of ourselves to others for the love of Christ: this is the sacrifice of our lay-priesthood.

This is the glorious adventure upon which we are embarked. Yet, how often we fail! Our morning resolutions seem so quickly shattered under one or the other of the day's poundings. We are men, not angels; we are the sons of a fallen Adam and we ache with the bruises of all our own falls. "Out of the depths I cry to thee . . ." and cry we must, but we must not become discouraged, for our major conquest is intended to be ourselves. All of the pounding to which we are submitted on the anvil of our daily lives is intended to form us in the image of Christ. Like iron which to be shaped must be heated and pounded, heated and pounded, so we are heated with the flames of grace and pounded under the hand of Him who would form us to perfection. "Be patient, then," St. Paul tells us, "while correction lasts; God is treating you as his children. Was there ever a son whom his father did not correct? . . . he does it for our good, to give us a share in that holiness which is his. For the time being, all correction is painful rather than pleasant; but afterwards, when it has done its work of discipline, it yields a harvest of good dispositions, to our great peace. Come then, stiffen the sinews of drooping hand, and flagging knee, and plant your footprints in a straight track, so that the man who goes lame may not stumble out of the path, but regain strength instead. Your aim must be peace with all men, and that holiness without which no one will ever see God." (Heb. 12:7, 10-14)

Under Christ, even our failures become a source of grace when we accept them in imitation of His humility, even our sufferings become a path to holiness when we ally them with His sufferings. All that we do and say, if it is done and said in Him is done and said perfectly, for true perfection is life in Christ.

There are many who would not classify themselves among the unbelievers, indeed they would be revolted at the suggestion, so comfortably entrenched are they in their religious habits. Yet our Lord saved his harshest castigation not for the unbelievers standing outside the Church, but for those warming themselves within: "cold or hot, I would thou wert one or the other. Being what thou art, luke-warm, neither cold nor hot, thou wilt make me vomit thee out of my mouth." (Apoc. 3:15-16) As a Christian, the father of the family cannot be mediocre. At the risk of being vomited out, he cannot be satisfied with a comfortable modicum of the spiritual life and, as the temper of the times would dictate, thrust aside all thought of the uncomfortable standard which Christ raises above him: the standard of His Cross. Those who preach a Christianity without the Cross fail to see that in order to reach heaven we must be, like our Lord, stretched on a cross.

Always before us we must keep His words: "you are to be perfect." And, examining our consciences, we must root out in regular confession all those failures in keeping that command. Only when we have through that grace conquered ourselves completely, defeated every malicious urge, routed out all the enemies of good within us; only when the goodness of God illumines every thought and action of ours, can we be said to be saints. Only then will we be the men God wants us to be. Only then will we be perfectly ourselves, because only then will we be able to say with St. Paul, "I am alive; or rather, not I; it is Christ that lives in me." (Gal. 2:20)

The Christian father must look before him to the ideal set up by Christ and then he must look to the weapons which Christ gave him in order that he may defeat the enemies of his growth and achieve that fullness for which his whole nature yearns: the Beatific Vision. Against those enemies the contemporary father has need for not merely the natural virtues of Aristotle's magnanimous man, but for the supernatural virtues of faith, hope and charity. The battle the father is waging is a spiritual battle, a battle on the supernatural level and one which can be won only with supernatural weapons.

How especially necessary the theological virtues are for the head of the family today! How, without supernatural faith, can a man be expected to stand up against the modern world's frontal assaults on the family?

The nation's economy and its thinking are oriented to the "four person family," with all that that means in the way of economic hardship and social disapproval for larger families. Older, larger homes are rapidly being demolished and replaced by smaller, new ones that do not permit any "extended" family life—such as caring for aged or infirm relatives, receiving foster children. Commodity merchants and media men encourage a "generation gap" mentality that strains even further the normally sensitive parent/child relationship. Enormous pressure placed on every head of a family to strive for material "security"; millions of dollars are spent inculcating the "insurance mentality" that looks on the future with dread. The ferment going on throughout the society and the world as a result of the constantly accelerating rate of social change; the attacks on "institutional Christianity"; the increasing acceptance of "drug culture" and "divorcing society" standards; the rising tide of violence and the steady increase in the number of those who are accepting the anti-life arguments of abortionists and euthanasiasts; all are factors which make almost daily demands on the father's trust in God and his willingness to follow the teachings of His Church.

It is in a time such as our own that the man of Faith, the household of the Faith, is truly revealed. For the times make continual demands on the Christian to reaffirm his faith not only in prayer, in words to God, but in his acceptance of God's will and his willingness to speak out both by words and deeds of the Faith that is in him.

Confronted by the possibility of nuclear war and the present actuality of harmful radioactive deposits in the bones of every child born since the beginning of the nuclear age; facing a world ripped with violence, atrocities and genocide; knowing his children will enter a world of growing totalitarianism, of human engineering and militarism; only the man with a lively hope can overcome the tendency to despair. Only such a man is armored for the adventure of paternity. Despite the deathly secularistic environment, despite the immensely more difficult task of protecting the innocence and purity of his children, the modern father—so well aware that he cannot succeed without God's help—must hope in God's goodness that He will provide the means for us and our children to obtain eternal life. This confidence in God on the part of the father will be one of the strongest reasons why his wife and children will find it easy to place confidence and trust in him.

Faith, hope—without these no father could long succeed in meeting the challenge of his calling, "but the greatest of them all is charity." (I Cor. 13:13) This often-quoted thirteenth chapter of the First Epistle to the Corinthians should be re-read frequently by the head of a family. It tells us that the faith that moves mountains is worthless without charity. It tells us that though we devote all our time and energy to feeding the poor, it is meaningless unless we have charity. St. Paul does not hesitate to say that though we submit to being burned at the stake, it merits us nothing if charity is lacking. On the other hand, the most humble act done in charity becomes a gift for the Lord. Charity transforms, transfigures all. All Christians know this, but the father of a family has special cause to meditate and act upon it since the greatest demands his daily life will make upon him will be demands upon his charity. In a sense, the father of a family has given himself away, gone to the stake, allowed himself to be consumed. If he lacks charity, if his giving is the cause of impatience, if it is rooted in self-interest or pride, if his sacrifice becomes the cause of private brooding or regret, then neither his giving nor his sacrifice count for much.

The father of a family has an unparalleled opportunity to root his entire life in his love of God. His heart can rejoice at the mere thought of each new child who, through him, will come to share the goodness of life. What, in a man without charity, is seen as an impingement upon his freedom, an intrusion upon his privacy, a diminishing of his self, is seen by the man who loves God as an opportunity for showing forth that love. More, his recognition of the way in which his family impinges upon him, far from being the source of any malice towards those who are a drain upon his resources and time, is seen as the way in which he is being formed in Christ. Such a man takes joy in receiving the living souls entrusted to him with patience and kindness, remembering the words of our Lord: "Believe me, when you did it to one of the least of my brethren here, you did it to me." (Matt. 25:40)

And our homes become schools of charity for all who live there, a charity that of its nature radiates outward, first to the receiving of all guests as Christ and then to the meeting with equal charity those who lack sympathy with our beliefs and our way of life. We can will the good of all our enemies. All those who are dedicated to ideals destructive of all we hold dear have a call upon our prayers. Perhaps through the love we hold for them, the example we set for them in Christ, we will one day be privileged to hear from them the words St. Augustine addressed to St. Ambrose: "I was not convinced by your arguments, but by the great love you showed me."

The evangelical counsels, too, have a place in the armory of the adventurer for Christ. If we are all called upon to be perfect, then we are called upon to follow, in keeping with our state in life, the counsels of perfection.

Nothing less than a radical spirit of poverty can cut a path to liberty through the jungle of commercialism in which we find ourselves. What less than a slicing away of the entangling undergrowth of senseless luxuries will allow us to find a sane balance in our daily lives? The most compelling need of our day, especially in America, a need more urgent than ever before in history, is for men who will re-enthrone Lady Poverty in their hearts. Such men will cease to seek money they have not earned, will not confuse luxuries with necessities, will use God's goods with a reverence that will startle and give pause to their compatriots who live by waste. One of the most powerful paradoxes of Christianity is this: that the truly poor man is the wealthiest of all men. A man in whom poverty is a living virtue, finds himself richer and freer than any of his wealthy neighbors. For the father of a family, who must make the important decisions concerning money, who must meet the needs of his family out of his resources of time and money, this virtue in its fullness is particularly indispensable. Only when he has detached himself from things, only when he has detached himself even from the consideration of time as somehow his own property will he be able to give fully. Then the giving will not only be easy, it will be a giving that finds him constantly replenished. The man who, like St. Francis, considers nothing his own, but all things God's to be used for God's purposes, will find himself enormously rich: all of creation becomes his.

Because poverty is linked in the American mind with destitution, it is little recommended to or by Americans; but Christian poverty is not destitution. None of us can escape having. Not even the vowed religious can escape having the clothes he wears, the tools he uses. But the vowed religious never forgets that what he is using or wearing does not belong to him, but is rather the property of God. Such people have liberated themselves from the attachment to earthly possessions which so easily drives a wedge between the heart and God. But one does not have to be a vowed religious to practice the virtue of poverty. In fact, even the very rich man can be poor in spirit, but for him it is most difficult.

"And Jesus looked round, and said to his disciples, With what difficulty will those who have riches enter God's kingdom! The disciples were amazed at his words; but Jesus gave them a second answer, My children, how hard it is for those who trust in riches to enter God's kingdom! It is easier for a camel to pass through a needle's eye, than for a man to enter the kingdom of God when he is rich. They were still more astonished; Why then, they said to themselves, who can be saved?" (Mark 10: 23-26) The apostles' incredulity at Christ's pronouncement was similar to our own. Their question shows how well they understood what our Lord was saying. For few men can detach themselves from their possessions—so strong is the hold material things have on our affections.

"Jesus fastened his eyes on them, and said, Such things are impossible to man's powers, but not to God's; to God, all things are possible." (Mark 10:27) It is, then, in response to grace that we can achieve that detachment necessary. Even the very rich man may hear God's call, respond to His graces and see his way clear to that self-denial which is fundamental to Christianity. "Poverty of spirit," Père Régamey says in his excellent book on this subject, "is at once the first word and the last of supernatural life. It opens the Kingdom of Heaven to us, and the supreme action of Charity is to become poor in God. Every stage of our progress is under the law of poverty."

The need for chastity in our society, no Christian can deny. Sexual immorality is so prevalent today that some think the term "immorality" only applies to sex! The contemporary insanity about sex, which no Christian needs be persuaded exists, is rooted not in an overestimation of sex as one at first might be tempted to believe, but in a gross underevaluation, a degradation of sex. Some look upon sex as a toy they are lucky enough to have, something they can play with; others see it as a commodity to be sold or as a means of selling commodities; some confuse it with love, while yet others treat it as a dirty little secret. All of these, even those who see sex as the greatest motivation in men's lives, are defiling sex. They are refusing to grant to the sexual that high reverence that is rightly its own. They will not honor it for what it is: an awesome gift of God to be used for His greatest work of creation.

The fact that the religious takes a vow of chastity and lives a celibate life has caused in some minds a confusion of chastity with celibacy. Chastity is, at root, a reverence for sex. The religious who vows to remain chaste in body and mind is offering up to God one of his greatest gifts, the use of his sexual power of procreation, that he may the more fully dedicate himself to God's work. The father of a family is by definition a non-celibate, but he must nonetheless be chaste. While he has been called to the married life, he is yet called upon to reverence sex for what it is. His chastity consists of his using his gift only within the marriage union, of recognizing in it not only a means of expressing his deepest commitment to another, but as one expression of his love for God, as, indeed, the core of that "great mystery" that is the sacrament of marriage. Chastity, then, is not, as some seem to believe, a mere negation of impurity, but a positive respect for the sacredness of sex. It is this awareness of the holiness of sex that will provide the father of the family with the resources whereby he can withstand and even help to counteract the distorters of sex who have tainted the very atmosphere of daily life. That high regard for the sexual act, that sense of its sacredness is as essential to the married man as to the single, if either is to keep his mind and heart clean in a society where dirt abounds. Our fidelity to our wives must be a fidelity rooted in a chaste mind, a chaste heart. Jesus was speaking to the multitude and not merely to his disciples when He said: "You have heard that it was said, Thou shalt not commit adultery. But I tell you that he who casts his eyes on a woman so as to lust after her has already committed adultery with her in his heart." (Matt. 5:27-28) Yet our advertising industry, our entertainment media, much of our periodical and book literature is overtly calculated to arouse just such adulterous thoughts in us! The father of the family here confronts an exterior enemy, but it is an enemy that can get through to him only because he bears within himself the wound of Original Sin. He will not overcome the exterior enemy until he has brought his interior enemy under discipline, chastened himself.

To some it may seem strange to talk of discipline within marriage, but it is to be hoped that the Christian man still realizes that, even within the marriage bond, he has need to discipline himself. The conjugal act should be truly an act of love; its meaning is reduced when it merely becomes a habit or a source of personal pleasure with no thought of the other party. On the other hand, at those times when abstinence from the marriage act is necessary, at times of illness or of childbirth, for instance, that abstinence should be rooted in love, too. The man who has mastery over his sexual powers, who has practiced restraint, is the man who will be capable of finding in those times of enforced abstinence a deepening of his love for his wife. What could so easily be a source of tension can be, if he relies upon the grace of God, a spring out of which flows a deeper love, a love expressing itself in the sacrifice of the normal expression of that love. Only the chaste man, however, only the man with the Christian awareness of the holiness of sex, can do this. Perhaps the lack of a true notion of what chastity entails in marriage is one of the reasons why even those who find it necessary to practice Rhythm find their times of abstinence times of a lessening of mutual love. They have not transfigured their mutual abstinence by charity, have not made of it a sacrifice which they offer up out of love, but have only tried to repress the normal flow of their love. And repression transfigures nothing, it only deforms.

The heart of the unchaste is a heart shrivelled and unclean. The heart of the chaste man is a pool of love. "Blessed are the clean of heart"; our Lord said, "they shall see God." (Matt. 5:8)

It is in obedience to Christ's call that the father of the family strives to purify himself. Obedient he must be, in imitation of Christ, to the demands of his vocation, even to the total sacrifice of self. Obedient above all to Christ's call of charity. And, as the father of a family, he is obedient to that first command of His Creator: "Increase and multiply . . ." Obedient to the call from God to be a co-creator with Him in the creation of new beings.

When God spoke to Moses from the burning bush, Moses asked His name: "And God said to Moses, I am the God who IS; thou shalt tell the Israelites, THE GOD WHO IS has sent me to you." (Exod. 3:14) Christian philosophy has never ceased to affirm that all existence is good because it participates in the existence of Him Who Is. For this reason, Christian philosophy has never ceased to maintain that it is better to be than not to be. The denial of the goodness of being, a denial once confined to certain Eastern philosophies, has today become common in our own society. It is a denial that expresses itself most eloquently in the strong campaign for abortion-on-demand, the rising voices of the euthanasia proponents. The killing of the unborn and the killing of the senile or the mentally ill are both fundamental denials of the goodness of being alive. In the face of such anti-life forces, the head of the family must draw deeply upon all his God given resources if he is to endure.

We have only sketched here most briefly the foremost among these resources, the theological virtues and the counsels of perfection. These depend, of course, upon prayer and the frequent reception of the sacraments of penance and the Holy Eucharist. It may be appropriate for us to recall here the Council of Trent's reiteration of the statement made by St. Augustine: "God does not command impossible things, but when He commands He warns us to do what can be done and to ask what cannot and gives you help so that you can."

God Himself has given the father a share in the enriching of the universe, of peopling not just this planet, but heaven itself. God hovers, waiting—the almighty God waiting upon a creature—for that creature to say "yes" to creation. And God makes that affirmation of the goodness of existence fruitful, takes the "yes" of the father for which he has been waiting and brings into the world a new being, a being of incalculable value because a being destined for eternal life with Him. And this treasure God entrusts to the father, giving him the commission to nurture, protect, educate and discipline this soul and prepare it for life in time and in eternity. This is the high adventure upon which the head of the family is embarked, this is his tremendous challenge today. He is called to share in the creative love of the Father, the sacrificial love of the Son, and the sanctifying love of the Holy Spirit. Through this work he is himself to be purified, to become a saint. Pope Pius XII, a truly Holy Father, told a group of midwives: "At the birth of the child, hasten, like the Romans of old, to place it in the arms of the father but with immeasurably greater spirit. For the ancient Romans this meant a recognition of paternity and the authority deriving from it: but in your case, it is an act of homage to and recognition of the Creator, an invoking of the Divine blessing, the duty of carrying out the office given by God with devotion and affection. If the Lord praises and rewards the faithful servant for the fruitful use of his five talents, what praise, what reward will He reserve for the father who has cherished and reared for Him the human life entrusted to him, a life worth more than all the gold and silver in the world."

Acknowledgments

The author and the publisher wish to make grateful acknowledgment to the following for the use of copyrighted materials in the present volume:

To His Eminence the Cardinal Archbishop of Westminster and to Sheed and Ward Inc., for their kind permission to quote extensively throughout this book from the Knox translation of the Sacred Scriptures. (*Old Testament*, vol. I, trans. by Msgr. Ronald Knox, Copyright 1948 by Sheed and Ward Inc., New York; *Old Testament*, vol. II, trans. by Msgr. Ronald Knox, Copyright 1950 by Sheed and Ward Inc., New York; *The New Testament*, trans. by Msgr. Knox, Copyright 1944 by Sheed and Ward Inc.)

To Sheed and Ward Inc. for kind permission to quote from *Poverty* by R. P. Regamey, O.P. (Copyright 1949 by Sheed and Ward Inc., New York) p. 164.

To the Dominican Friars of Hawkesyard Priory in Great Britain for kind permission to quote from *Life of the Spirit*, vol. XIV, Nos. 158-159, August-September 1959, p. 54.

To The America Press for kind permission to quote from: Pope Pius XII, *On the Sacred Liturgy* (New York: The America Press, 1948) p. 88; Pope Pius XII, *The Mystical Body of Christ* (New York: The America Press, 1955) p. 45; and Pope Pius XI, *Christian Education of Youth* (New York: The America Press, 1936) p. 9.

To G. P. Putnam's Sons for kind permission to quote from *Waiting for God* by Simone Weil (New York: G. P. Putnam's Sons, 1951) p. 114.

To the Catholic Truth Society of London for kind permission to quote from *The Pope Speaks to Mothers* by Pope Pius XII (London: The Catholic Truth Society, 1941) pp. 6-7.

To the Paulist Press for kind permission to quote from *Moral Questions Affecting Married Life* by Pope Pius XII (New York: The Paulist Press, 1951) p. 8.

Let's hear it for

THE HEAD OF THE FAMILY

"This book will so uplift the men who read it that they will be better men, better fathers and husbands for having read it."

The Way

". . . what it means to be the father of a family. Many a man will rediscover in these pages the inherent dignity of this state of life."

America

"*The Head of the Family* . . . creates a penetrating and large-screen view of fatherhood today."

The Sign

". . . the author thinks that the heads of families are 'the great adventurers of the modern world.' . . . Some fathers, perhaps many, will be able to meet that challenge better if they read this enjoyable book."

Worship

". . . candid treatment of the psychological and spiritual roles of the father as creator, lover, breadwinner, teacher and saint."

Ave Maria

". . . devout study of man's role as husband and father, describing a high concept of man fulfilling his destiny within the family relationships."

The Lutheran

"This is an excellent book, a man's book."

Marriage

"*The Head of the Family* . . . should be read by all laymen who are striving to live the Christian life. . . ."

The Catholic World

"This is a virile book. . . . Reading *The Head of the Family* will benefit fathers seeking guidance in their 'great adventure.'"

The Catholic Messenger